Last Chance to Avoid Extinction

By Renee Sonia Rotto

Last Chance to Avoid Extinction

Table of Contents

Forward

"The planet isn't going anywhere, we are. We're going away… Pack up your shit folks, we're going away. And we won't leave much of a trace, thank God for that. Maybe a little Styrofoam, maybe… a little Styrofoam, the planet will be here and we'll be long gone, just another failed mutation, just another closed end biological mistake, an evolutionary cultisack. The planet will shake us off like a bad case of fleas, a surface nuisance."
-- George Carlin

Species come and go, that is to say, most species go. In fact, scientists estimate that over 99% of all species that have ever inhabited Earth are now extinct. There have been five major mass extinction events since life began on this planet, with most occurring naturally; prior to Homo sapiens walking the Earth. While mass extinction is a relatively rare event, isolated extinction is quite common among species.

Why should we be concerned about the pattern of extinction or the extinction of other species? Because Homo sapiens are not immune to extinction–and through the study of past extinction events we may discover how we can avoid the extinction of our own species. Also the single extinction of some species can create a "chain of extinction," which commonly happens with *keystone species*.

Keystone species play a major role in maintaining the balance of all other species in their ecosystem. These species have the potential, if their numbers become low enough, to trigger a sudden collapse in not only their own ecosystem but this collapsing, culminates the beginning of the end of the cycle that provides human beings with food.

One such species is plankton. If the plankton population suddenly plummets, so do the fish and our food supply will diminish right along with them! Researchers in California are fearful that global warming may be causing the decrease in plankton that is occurring throughout the entire northern Pacific Ocean. Some scientists even warn that the loss could already be permanent. This will lead to devastating changes. Scientists recently predicted the total collapse of all types of edible fish in the ocean by the year of 2050. Of course, this prediction is not based solely on the loss of plankton alone, but also takes into account other factors such as pollution, commercial over fishing and the loss of diversity of fish species.

Regardless of human behavior it is acknowledged that at least twenty-five species go extinct every single day. Only recently, have scientists become alarmed at the higher rate of recent extinction and begun to estimate the trajectory of bio-diversity that might have taken place without human influence.

What had begun as a feeble attempt to control nature through selective breeding practices has morphed into harvesting genetically modified plants and animals, carcinogens in our food, water, and buildings along with every facet of our environment. Humans are altering life on this planet with their technology of the great and small. Man with all his brainpower, has proclaimed himself God of all creatures, forgetting that, the odds of avoiding extinction are not in his favor, and that mankind may soon find himself on the endangered species list.

This book will attempt to outline the many possible causes of why humans will become extinct in the very near future unless we utilizes our brainpower to its fullest potential and are capable of finding solutions that integrate with the natural order of this planet. Our new technologies are exponentially changing the environment of planet Earth. By doing so, humans may have only two possibilities to avoid extinction. If like any other species, Homo sapiens are unable to adapt to the new environment, we too will become extinct or we will have no other choice but to escape Earth.

Understanding what the future holds for mankind could be as simple as recognizing the patterns of past mass extinction events and how changes in our environment will affect our lives, health and longevity as a species. It will provide a heads up, on what to expect in the coming years. Whether or not Homo sapiens will succumb to the fate of over 99% of species that came before; only time will tell. Which path will we choose to stay alive, or is it already too late for Homo sapiens?

Overpopulation

"4.5 Earths would be required to support a global population living like an average resident of the U.S."
-- Jim Leape, WWF International

Overpopulation will become a serious problem in the coming years. According to the U.S. Census Bureau, population projection expects that we will reach a whapping 9.2 billion of us by the year 2050. Some other predictions are estimating the population in 2050 will be as high as 11 billion. Wrap your head around this: every 20 minutes the human population grows by about 3,000 people. Do our vastly increasing numbers mean that we are doomed as a species? Is there still something we can do to eliminate overpopulation?

One answer seems obvious. We as a species need to stop having so many children. For decades scientists have warned of the dangers of overpopulation and suggested reducing the family unit size to one or two children per family. Humans have long passed the point, of needing to be fruitful and multiply. It took us roughly about 200,000 years since man first appeared on Earth, to populate to one billion. The second billion came only one hundred years afterwards. Presently, we add one billion people to our planet every twelve years.

The most dramatic increases of population come from the poorest and least urbanized areas around the globe. With that said, it is also estimated that some 680 million people are chronically hungry on this planet. Food and water scarcities are destined to increase even more quickly as the world's population races to unsustainable levels.

Unfortunately, only 17% of the world's population lives in industrialized countries. Africa and Asia have a projected population growth that is set to exceed one-third of the world's population. This is important news for less urbanized countries along with the need for education on the use of birth control. Birth control is one factor but not the only issue that should be addressed. There is a huge discrepancy between needs and services available. Consider this; the richest 20% of humanity consume 86% of all goods and services and the poorest fifth of the world consumes only 1.3% of those goods and services.

Population growth of this magnitude cannot be sustained. It will eventually cause devastating effects for everyone. It will have life altering affects in all areas of our lives. Problems such as global warming, pollution and raising levels of atmospheric carbon dioxide will only be exacerbated by our overpopulation. The Global Footprint Network and the World Wide Fund for Nature has stated that we have already reached and exceeded the carrying capacity for our planet. The populations' continued growth would cause even greater demands for resources that are already being stretched to capacity and are already in short supply even in industrial countries.

Anyone who has been paying attention to prices at the grocery store can attest to the sharp increases for the basic necessities of life. Necessities such as food, water, minerals and energy will be depleted even further in the very, near future. Fresh water supplies are already running low worldwide; a crisis that will only worsen as the temperature rises and the population increases around the globe.

Overpopulation of the planet will change many things that might otherwise seem unrelated. The population increase will have a negative effect on everyone but especially developing countries, as water supplies diminish, wiping out water that was once available for the irrigation of crops. It is estimated that by the year 2020, 135 million people may lose their land as a result of soil degradation. The good old days of a nomad migrating culture are long gone. There are few untouched virgin lands for us to uncover. Drought, thoughtless commercial farming techniques and improper crop rotation are often responsible for the loss of farmable land. Factor in, an increase in population growth and it becomes clear how our very numbers adhere to the possible demise of our own species.

The End of the Never Ending Supply

With the predictable jump in our population some things will no doubt be in short supply in the coming years. Other than food and water, energy is at the top of the list of essential needs. But no matter how much we plan to, "drill baby drill," at some point, oil will no longer be an option. This is not a difficult concept to understand. There is an *end to the never-ending supply*. While governments fight over the existing supplies of fossil fuels, no immediacy seems evident to find replacements. Instead of investing in renewable sources of power, for the most part, we are deniers of the end of the fossil fuel supply.

There have been many ideas developed for the creation of free energy. Throughout history there have been inventors who have invented such things, only to have their inventions suppressed. Instead of praise for their efforts, these altruistic individuals were often left to languish—their fate apprehended within the confines of the walls of a prison cell. The promise of cold fusion, aquaponics, solar and wind power along with many other recent discoveries will not be allowed to truly go forward without global efforts. To change and make the investments necessary must be adhered to by all nations. In order to find free, safe, reusable energy forms for the planet, it takes not only a village, but also the planets' cooperation. If we don't, we will become a society that will literally be set back to the dark ages.

Soon the end of the never-ending supply will begin to become apparent; if you haven't noticed it has already begun. We still have oil supplies that can be extracted, but it won't be easily done. What's left will cost us dearly to refine. But gas for your car is only the tip of the iceberg. Everything will cost more as we reach the *end of the never-ending supply*. With all of the hazards that overpopulation brings, it is still within our control to change. Overpopulation is only one of many threats to Homo sapiens' existence. Some of the most ominous threats will come from nature itself.

Forces of Nature

"Even with all our technology and the inventions that make modern life so much easier than it once was, it takes just one big natural disaster to wipe all that away and remind us that, here on Earth, we're still at the mercy of nature".
--Neil deGrasse Tyson

Extinction from natural causes is a common phenomenon. In the past when one species died, the rate of extinction was balanced by the evolution of a new species. Anthony Barnosky, a paleobiologist at the University of California said in a startling prediction, that the current rate of extinction is 1,000 times the natural rate. Human factors and activities are responsible for the elevated extinction rates of many species.

Because human activities are so closely tied to the ecosystem, what we do is an antecedent to catastrophes in nature. Everyone by now has heard of the connection between global warming and fierce storms. This includes hurricanes, typhoons and blizzards. The hotter the planet becomes along with more pollution in our atmosphere, results in acid rain. When the chemicals sulfur dioxide and/or nitrogen oxide, gets absorbed in the clouds and fall back to Earth as rain or snow it increases the acidity of the soil. This in turn affects plant life, with the run off flowing into larger bodies of water. When the pH of a lake drops below 4.8, the plants and animals in that lake are at risk of death. It has been estimated that about 50,000 lakes in the U.S. and Canada have pH levels below normal, with several hundred others having a pH level too low to sustain any aquatic life at all.

The forces of nature that cause extinction come in many flavors. The planet Earth has survived many devastating natural catastrophes with only a small fraction of its species having avoided extinction. Our little blue planet has endured massive earthquakes, volcanic eruptions, hurricanes, plate tectonics, sunspots, continual drifts, magnetic storms, cosmic rays and the magnetic reversal of the poles. Comets, asteroids and meteors have bombarded Earth over hundreds of thousands of years. Earth has overcome worldwide floods, tidal waves, fires, erosion and recurring ice ages.

All of these catastrophic natural disasters have the capacity to take out huge portions of species at any given time but some natural calamities are potentially even more deadly than others. Global warming or climate change will have a devastating effect for many, many species. Along with the impact of rising temperatures some of the most serious natural threats to the extinction of Homo sapiens are climate change, gamma rays and the flood basalt.

Climate Change

"Climate change is a terrible problem, and it absolutely needs to be solved. It deserves to be a huge priority."
--Bill Gates

Life on earth must be pretty darn fragile if a few degrees of temperature change can wipe out thousands of species, right? It's not that our little blue planet will just become slightly warmer that's the problem, it's all the problems that rising temperatures generate. Besides droughts and less food and water for everyone, it increases ocean warming and hastens the melting of glaciers and ice sheets. This in turn raises the sea level, increases carbon dioxide causing a "greenhouse effect" that changes our atmosphere and the acidity of lakes and oceans.

Data from the National Oceanic & Atmospheric Administration, the current level of CO_2 in the world's atmosphere is around 393 parts per million or (ppm). In 1979, the CO_2 levels were approximately around 336 parts per million. Before the industrial age the CO_2 levels were around 280 parts per million. This rise in Carbon Dioxide is worsened by the fact that 50% of the World's tropical rain forests have been cleared or degraded, which reduces our chances of reducing the CO_2 levels naturally. According to the Food and Agriculture Organization of the United Nations, 13 million hectares of forest are being lost per year. That's equivalent to 36 football fields per minute.

For those who want to resist the idea of climate change, there is bad news: climate change is real. Heat waves are becoming longer and hotter. Flooding and heavy rains are becoming more frequent and extremes in the weather are becoming more intense and widespread. We are releasing greenhouse gasses into the atmosphere at an increasingly rapid rate.

The seemingly insignificant rise of a few degrees has actually been proceeding at an unprecedented level over the past 1,300 years. Scientists are literally now able to see the big picture as they collect information about the planet and the climate from satellites and other technology. The global sea level has risen about 17 centimeters in the last century. Additionally, the rate within the last decade has nearly doubled that of the previous century. This new data confirms what has been suspected and is just one more piece of evidence; climate change is real.

Scientists are now able to view raising global sea levels and shrinking ice sheets. Data from NASA's Gravity Recovery and Climate Experiment show Greenland lost 150 to 250 cubic kilometers (36 to 60 cubic miles) of ice per year between 2002 and 2006. Antarctica lost about 152 cubic kilometers or (36 cubic miles) of ice between 2002 and 2005. There is also a decline in Arctic Sea ice, in respects to the extent as well the thickness over the last several decades. Scientific imagery in space gives us a view of the disappearing snowcap of Mount Kilimanjaro and allows us to watch glaciers retreating almost everywhere around the world. Glaciers in the Alps, Andes, Himalayas, Rockies, Alaska and Africa are right now being reduced to acidic pools of surface ocean water, right before our eyes. The carbon dioxide that is absorbed by the upper layers of the ocean is increasing by about 2 billion tons per year. What does this sea raising level mean? The short answer is less viable land for our overpopulated planet.

The scientific evidence that planet Earth is warming up is unequivocal but it still may be possible to turn things around if not to at least halt its progression. World leaders are beginning to wake up to the dangers of climate change and attempting to reduce greenhouse emissions to pre-industrial levels. In fact, in spite of squabbles and denials revolving around global warming, there is evidence that Governments are actually quite aware of its ramifications.

At an international symposium held in Ghent, Belgium back in 2010 scientists asserted that "manipulation of climate through modification of Cirrus clouds is neither a hoax nor a conspiracy theory." Further, these types of attempts to manipulate the weather are "fully operational." They are continuing without public knowledge or agreement of what is being sprayed into our atmosphere. After all, trying to modify the climate is a relatively new area of scientific study. Governments have denied for years, it's undertaking. All over the world, people began looking up to the skies and noticing emissions coming from planes that formed circles, lines, crisscross patterns, grid like patterns and parallel stripes and wondered what it was that these planes were dropping into the atmosphere.

They are called chemtrails. They are governments' little darlings, to test if humans can artificially alter the weather. Investigations of chemtrails have shown high levels of aluminum salts, barium, polymer fibers, thorium and silicon carbide in the atmosphere and land. Test results on chemtrails have returned positive results for these chemicals and also bacteria, viruses and mold.

Recent sprayings have hampered the health of many in their vicinity. Depending on a person's immune system and general health, some people have experienced pneumonia or respiratory symptoms. Other people report mental confusion and depression following these sprayings. It has also been reported that many deadly and toxic pathogens have been found. Some of these toxic pathogens are the same bio-engineered pathogens that 45% of the veterans who came down with Gulf War illness had.

Chemtrails are turning out to be another covert plan to clean up the universe. Proponents of chemtrails have pointed to congressional record as proof of a cover-up. In 2001 Congressman, Dennis Kucinich introduced legislation to permanently prohibit the basing of weapons in space. Within that same legislation, chemtrails was listed as one of a number of weapons that would be banned. The bill was never passed and chemtrail theorists believe that congressional record, in-itself, is proof positive of the governments' knowledge of chemtrails. Evidently, governments are quite aware of our rapidly changing climate and in their own way, have been attempting to alter it. But some scientists are fearful it may already be too late. So for all practical purposes, expect at the very least, some major fallout because of global warming. If it doesn't take us out completely, it will definitely wane our numbers.

Global warming will bring down the population. For the survivors of climate change, life won't resemble life as it is today. Many species will disappear at an exponential rate and many of us will not make it due to famine, drought and shortages of all varieties. If we are able to at least halt the progression of global warming, we as a species will have a chance to face off with the other two most dangerous forces of natural extinction events.

Gamma Ray Bursts

"In general, the objects in the universe that are very high-energy objects, or the processes that are high-energy processes, will radiate more in the short wavelength range towards the gamma rays or the x-ray.
--Claude Nicollier

Within the universe there are various energy forms. Radiation is the wave energy, which is produced by electromagnetic forces such as, alpha rays, beta rays and gamma rays. These high-energy particles travel through space and bombard Earth's ozone layer. Alpha rays are the weakest wave in the electromagnetic spectrum. A sheet of paper or human skin can easily block alpha rays. The second form of radioactive particles, is the beta ray, which can be blocked by aluminum, but the gamma ray can only be blocked by lead.

Gamma rays have the smallest wavelength and are generated by radioactive atoms and nuclear explosions. Cosmic gamma rays can collide with other particles and be annihilated with its anti-particles. As particles and elements then begin to undergo radioactive decay these charged particles are accelerated throughout space.

Gamma rays are the most toxic of the radioactive particles within the universe because they easily penetrate through the skin and kills living cells. Normally alpha rays, beta rays and gamma rays penetrate and are absorbed at differing depths within the Earth's atmosphere. The ozone layer that surrounds the Earth helps protect us from these radioactive wave particles and help to prevent the ultraviolet light from reaching the Earth's surface. If the hole in the ozone layer over Antarctica keep getting larger due to climate change, Earth will have little protection against killer gamma rays bursts. Without the protection from the ozone layer the high-energy form of radiation from a gamma ray blast would be so dangerous it would kill most life forms within a very, short time. Even those who survived the initial gamma ray blast would suffer from mutations and so would their DNA.

Some gamma rays are from natural sources here on Earth. This includes gamma decay from naturally occurring radioisotopes. These are when gamma rays are produced from natural sources such as lighting, terrestrial gamma ray flashes and radioactive decay. However, the most threatening gamma rays are produced at the hottest places in the universe. They are called gamma ray bursts. Gamma ray bursts are the result of violent events in space. The death of a massive star called, Supernova explosions, pulsars, black holes and neutron stars all create celestial gamma rays. When the core of a massive star collapses, streams of high-energy radiation are produced.

A gamma ray blast travels across vast distances of the universe with most of their energy being released in just seconds, as decay begins. They are brief but intense. Explosions that produce gamma ray bursts occur in every region of space with nearly daily regularity. The 'afterglow' of these powerful explosions could be 10 billion light years away, traveling near the speed of light or it could happen much closer to home.

Gamma rays can travel much farther than alpha rays or beta rays. Because of their penetrating power and ability to travel great distances it would be considered a catastrophic emergency if Earth were ever hit directly from a gamma ray burst. Today scientists believe that 440 million years ago a gamma ray burst may have been the cause for the second worst mass extinction events on Earth—and it could happen again.

What would happen if Earth were suddenly hit with a gamma ray blast? Here on Earth we wouldn't be aware of a heat wave or a shock wave as the invisible gamma rays burst beams, hit us. The first thing you would see would be a very bright flash in the sky, then the whole sky would turn completely white—as gasses glow when they are hit by gamma rays. This would begin the destruction of the ozone layer, as the beam would blast apart molecules of our two principal gasses: oxygen and nitrogen. Single atoms of each of these elements would be free to recombine as nitrogen oxide.

UV waves would soar by 80%, as nitrogen dioxide would cover the sky in a gray haze. The Earth would become dark, as sunlight would be blocked out. There would be a global cooling that would last for months afterwards.

A simulation using a new computer model shows us how a gamma ray burst aimed directly at Earth could deplete the ozone layer, cause acid rain, and initiate global cooling from as far as 6,500 light years away from Earth. After a gamma ray burst only about 10% of the Earth's population would be wiped out but the Earth would only be able to support about 10% of its remaining population. It is estimated that in just 85 minutes after a gamma ray blast the Earth would have suffered enough damage for it to take a decade to recover.

With around 100,000 neutron stars within our observable visual field, nobody knows when they might collide and create a gamma ray burst. Gamma ray blasts might seem more like science fiction, yet these "death rays" in space are a daily occurrence. Although a direct hit from a gamma ray burst is not likely within the scope of one's lifetime, the evidence is clear that we can never be completely safe. What happened before, can certainly happen again; and in fact, will definitely occur again given enough time.

As scary as a potential gamma ray burst is, there is one other natural killer that has the potential to do much more damage. It has been identified as the cause of a mass extinction event that wiped out at least 95% of all species here on Earth in the past. But this grievous nightmare will not come from outer space, but from deep inside the Earth instead. It is the unstoppable process that could threaten our species existence. The name for this unstoppable force is the flood basalt.

The Flood Basalt

"If you ever drop your keys into a river of lava, man, just forget them...because they're gone!"
--Jack Handey

The most devastating extinction event the Earth has ever known happened during the Permian-Triassic boundary and was responsible for the extinction of at least 90% of all living things. The massive volcanic eruption event known as a flood basalt eruption is believed to be the cause or at least in part. The main question is, whether the step-like, hill formation, which we call the Siberian Traps, was in itself responsible for this mass extinction event or was there a larger event involved, such as an asteroid?

About 250 million years ago the biggest and most horrific extinction event on Earth began. It certainly may have been a chain reaction that was lethal enough to kill almost every living creature. The extinction event, that was called the 'Great Dying,' probably began with thousands of miles of lava bursting up from deep inside the Earth's crust. In the end hundreds of thousands of miles of Siberia caught fire and continued to burn for over a million years, raising the global temperature. It has been hypothesized that the rising temperatures of the sea triggered the sudden release of methane from methane clathrate compounds buried in the oceans causing further warming.

Methane is a powerful greenhouse gas. Once this process had begun—it in effect initiated a runaway progression of destabilization that drastically altered the ocean environment. As acidification took hold in the oceans, the global temperatures were still rising. The huge injection of these greenhouse gases pushed the global temperatures up 10 degrees. Calculations of seawater temperatures indicate that ocean water may have exceeded 105 degrees over the next tens of thousands of years. This excessive heating of the oceans exceeded the thermal tolerance for most of marine life, essentially taking out over 95% of all marine species.

Flood basalt eruptions have occurred on continental scales and have erupted at random intervals throughout history. They have been

18

termed "Curtain of Fire" as fluid gas-poor basaltic magma rises up through fissures in the Earth's crust. One explanation of why flood basalt eruptions happen is, that it could be a combination of effects such as, continental rifting, and decompression melting in conjunction with mantles pluming. If there is a link between flood basalt events and mass extinction events, it may be due to the environmental impact of the gases released.

Whatever their cause, the flood basalt is poorly understood, but it has the ability to flow thousands of miles, killing all that it touches. Could a flood basalt eruption cause a domino effect that begins the next mass extinction? Are humans smart enough to find a way to adapt to what nature throws at us? Even if our species finds a way to circumvent this potential mass extinction event, we still won't be out of the woods. Unlike other species that have ruled the Earth, Homo sapiens are altering the very fabric of all living things on the planet by modifying our food, water and manufactured goods. The next threat of extinction for Homo sapiens comes from the man made carcinogens that we ourselves are creating within our environment.

Poison in our food and water

"We don't have to save the world. The world is big enough to look after itself. What we have to be concerned about is whether or not the world we live in will be capable of sustaining us in it."
--Douglas Adams

Anyone who is familiar with the statement, "you are what you eat." should be suspicious of what is ending up on our kitchen table. If you're eating prepared foods or processed foods there's at least a 90% chance you've been consuming genetically modified [GM] foods. They are in our grains, fruits, vegetables and meats, without labeling to warn us of their presence. Monsanto's website states, "There is no need for, or value in testing the safety of GM foods in humans."

Despite what the creators of genetically modified foods say about the safety of these foods, their claims are primarily without much scientific scrutiny. The fact is that no one really knows what the repercussions of eating these *Franken-foods* are. Some scientists believe that eating GM foods could give you cancer.

One leading expert in tissue diseases, Dr. Stanley Ewen a consultant histopathologist in Scotland says the cauliflower virus used as a vector in spawning GM foods could increase the risk of stomach and colon cancers. A statement released by American Academy of Environmental Medicine stated, "There is more than a casual association between GM foods and adverse health effects. There is a causation." The Academy warns that the public should avoid genetically modified foods.

Many other studies report incidents of a wide variety of health problems associated with genetically modified foods. Some of these include: immune dysfunction, insulin disorders, food allergies, accelerated aging, organ damage and reproductive disorders. Still other research indicates that genetic abnormalities of genetically modified foods may transfer to bacteria in the human gut. This is another indication that the dangerous effects of GM foods remain paramount even long after the food has been consumed.

Crops that were modified to produce the pesticide Bt, (which has been approved for human consumption in the U.S.) have been fed to farm animals with shocking results. Animals left to graze on the GM crops died by the thousands while other animals grazing on a non-GM version were unharmed. Autopsies of the dead animals revealed black patches on the livers and intestines. These animals also suffered from internal bleeding and other signs of Bt poisoning.

New research and understanding of the actuality of what we're consuming is beginning to rock the GM boat. It turns out that what we eat is more than just vitamins and protein; our bodies are absorbing information from what we eat. Chinese researchers have found small pieces of rice that contain ribonucleic acid (RNA) in the blood and organs of the humans who eat rice. The research team, from Nanjing University has shown that this genetic material can and does bind to receptors in human liver cells and influences the uptake of cholesterol from the blood.

This particular type of RNA is called microRNA or MiRNAs and has been studied extensively over the last decade. It has been implicated as a player in several diseases including cancer, Alzheimer's, and diabetes.

The usual function of shutting down or turning off certain genes has sparked another branch of scientific study known as epigenetics. The new Chinese research has shown us how ingested plant miRNA is surviving digestion and influencing human cell function. While the Chinese study had initially nothing to do with genetically modified foods, the work provides a pathway of understanding of how these new foods could influence human health in unanticipated ways.

Monsanto has claimed that human toxicology testing was unwarranted based on the doctrine of something called "substantial equivalence." According to the substantial equivalence notion, a comparison is only necessary to investigate the end product of the DNA expression. The new DNA of a tomato injected with a gene from a fish is not considered a threat in any other way.

Even as far back as 1999, a group of scientists had written a letter to the journal *Nature* titled "Beyond Substantial Equivalence," which called substantial equivalence "a pseudo-scientific concept that is inherently anti-scientific because it was created primarily to provide an excuse for not requiring biochemical or toxicological tests."

One of the latest inclusions to be added to the GM family of foods comes from a company called AquaBounty. The company is promoting a genetically modified salmon that can grow at an expeditious rate. The USDA has given half a million dollars of taxpayer's money to produce the supposedly sterile fish, despite overwhelming opposition. AquaBounty claims to have launched us into a "blue revolution," bringing together biological sciences and molecular technology. Their next endeavors will be trout, tilapia, shrimp and lobster.

Why should this bother you? Besides the nauseating idea of eating plants and animals grown in a laboratory with spliced genes of another species, using a vector of a virus to inject genetic material—there is evidence that these *Franken-foods* are being infiltrated into our environment on a colossal scale. What may have been intended to be sterile or contained has the potential to propagate or escape its confines. Genetically modified seed can turn up wherever the wind blows much to the dismay of the organic farmer. But even that being said, it is certainly not the end of the story. New evidence is revealing that genetically modified crops are leaving behind their DNA in the soil that they occupy. The genetically modified foods' DNA remains there in the ground for soil bearing animals and microorganisms to feed on. From there is goes up the food chain, gradually making its way back to its creator.

Many countries are trying hard to ban GM foods but that may be difficult on a global scale. In some respects, the genie is already out of the bottle. Perhaps the only hope we have to rid ourselves of GM foods is to stop it cold and hope the Earth can self-correct; eradicating these foods as a mutation gone horribly wrong.

In school we are taught that the human body is made up of 80% water. In most cities across the U.S. what runs out of the faucet as the most necessary fluid for human existence is tainted with the toxic waste product, fluoride.

Fluoride has been regarded as an environmental pollutant before 1945. At that time fluoride was responsible for many lawsuits against the aluminum industry and the phosphate fertilizer industry. It destroyed crops and killed animals. It was found that fluoride was a toxic environmental pollutant that had to be reduced or eliminated from the environment. Even though it had to be disposed of, its manufacturers would have to pay millions to dispose of it properly. So how did they decide to get rid of fluoride? They put it in the municipal water supply.

Christopher Bryson, examines the background of fluoridation in his book, "*The Fluoride Deception*" and said that at the time research on fluoride's safety was either suppressed or not conducted at all. He also said fluoridation in the water supply was not a triumph of medical science but a United States Government spin. The industry not only made millions from selling this pollutant to water companies and toothpaste companies but also saved billions on what would have been required to clean it up.

Since 1999 over 60 U.S. communities have rejected water fluoridation proposals along with 98% of Western Europe. To this day, about 60% of the United States have fluoride in their water supply even though water fluoridation does not have FDA approval.

A study conducted at the University of Iowa reported that 71% of more than 300 soft drinks contained 0.60 ppm of fluoride. Fluoride can be found in processed foods, fresh fruits and vegetables and vitamins and mineral supplements. Teflon is coated with fluoride and cooking with it presents special concerns for bird lovers, as the fumes released from cooking with Teflon have been known to kill them.

Fluoride is also in drugs and antibiotics. In 1990 about 220 fluorinated pharmaceutical drugs hit the market with some 1,500 still being developed. The drugs Prozac and Paxil are fluorinated drugs. In the past fluoride compounds were added to the drinking water of prisoners to keep them docile. Fluoride is even in some appetite suppressants, antacids, antihistamines and arthritis medicines.

What are the effects of fluoride? Fluoride causes diseases such as Down's syndrome, kidney, heart, bone and liver problem. It has been linked with more than 10,000 cancer deaths every year in the United States. There is an association with aluminum fluoride and Alzheimer's disease. Aluminum compounds are frequently added to water along side with fluoride. By itself aluminum is not absorbed by the body. But when fluoride is present, the two-form aluminum fluoride, which is easily absorbed. Aluminum fluoride produces lesions to the brain that are similar to Alzheimer's and dementia.

With our most basic need being compromised on a daily basis, the very fabric of what Homo sapiens are made of, begins to unravel. Earth is apt to descend to a cesspool of man-made carcinogens that will haunt generations to come. Toxic materials are everywhere. We have incorporated carcinogens in every facet of our environment, not only in our food and water. If the human form can somehow override the injurious meals and cocktails we devour daily, can it also fight off the long list of poisons that surround us? It is not only what we eat and drink that has potential to be fatal to us; it is in almost everything else that we come into contact with.

Manufacturing Carcinogens

"The landscape of carcinogens is not static either. We are chemical apes: having discovered the capacity to extract, purify, and react molecules to produce new and wondrous molecules, we have begun to spin a new chemical universe around ourselves. Our bodies, our cells, our genes are thus being immersed and reimmersed in a changing flux of molecules—pesticides, pharmaceutical drugs, plastics, cosmetics, estrogens, food products, hormones, even novel forms of physical impulses, such as radiation and magnetism. Some of these, inevitably, will be carcinogenic. We cannot wish this world away; our task, then, is to sift through it vigilantly to discriminate bona fide carcinogens from innocent and useful bystanders."
--Siddhartha Mukherjee, *The Emperor of All Maladies*

Every year Americans generate 250 million tons of garbage. Within 12-month period humans generate enough hazardous waste to fill the New Orleans Superdome 1,500 times over. According to the Environmental Protection Agency, the United States has 3,091 active landfills and over 10,000 municipal landfills. All of these landfills create hazardous air emissions that eventually leach into our ground water.

Chemicals that are used in industry create dangerous forms of waste. The amount of these types of chemicals has risen over the years as the world has become more industrialized. There are more than 80,000 different chemicals that are used in industries worldwide. In addition to that, 1,500 new chemicals are invented each year. Back in 2000, it was reported that at least 82% of landfill cells had leaked into our groundwater. It is also noted that as of 1992, 14 billion pounds of trash had been dumped into the ocean around the world as well.

Toxic materials such as PVCs that are used for the backing of carpets have dominated the industry for over 30 years, mainly because it is a cheap, durable material. Unfortunately, it is also a human carcinogen. PVCs are routinely used in a variety of consumer products, including toys, sporting goods and clothing. When PVC is incinerated it gives off dioxin emissions that cause an alarming amount of health related illnesses. Other hazardous materials such as small particles from degraded plastic bags and PCBs get into our water and get ingested by filter feeding marine animals and then these toxins get passed up the food chain to humans.

Formaldehyde is a commonly used carcinogen. It is used as a preservative in cosmetics. Most of us can recall seeing specimens preserved in formaldehyde from a biology class or have heard that formaldehyde is used during the embalming process of the dead. But we can also find formaldehyde in shampoo, conditioners, shower gel and liquid hand washing soap. Even products designed for children have formaldehyde. Formaldehyde has been shown to cause cancer in animals and is suspected of causing cancer in humans. It has been known to trigger asthma attacks and cause burning sensations to the eyes and throat. While humans exposure is considered elevated at (above 0.1 parts per million) some people may be more sensitive than others.

Lead in paint has been tied to a reduced IQ, learning disabilities, hearing loss and behavior problems in children. Children are more susceptible to the effects of even low levels of lead because their bodies are still developing. Some of the most sensitive parts of the body are the central nervous system along with the kidneys and the blood. Although lead paint is no longer used its remnants remain in landfills everywhere.

Benzene is another chemical which is considered a carcinogen. It is present in cigarettes, gasoline, some industrial processes and auto exhaust. Benzene is also found in certain consumer goods and has been linked to leukemia. This carcinogen is tightly regulated in the United States although thresholds for benzene exposure have never been established.

Asbestos has been a known carcinogen that increases the risk of lung cancer and mesothelioma. It has been used commercially since the late 1800s. Asbestos is used in a wide range of industries because its fibers are resistant to heat, fire and chemicals. Building and construction industries have used it to strengthen cement and plastics as well as for insulation, sound absorption, roofing, and fireproofing. Shipbuilders have utilized it to insulate hot water pipes, steam pipes and boilers. The automotive industry uses asbestos to make clutch pads and brake pads. Asbestos has been used in adhesives, paints, and plastics ceiling and floor tiles and is still found in older buildings.

Humans are manufacturing carcinogens at break-neck speed with all our electronic toys. The EPA reports that over 112 computers a day are discarded within the U.S. alone. It is estimated that electronic waste could rise by as much as 500% over the next decade. Electronic waste from equipment produces dangerous chemicals such as mercury, lead, cadmium, beryllium and flame retardant. Think about this: a pre-flat screen television contains 4.360 chemicals within it, and a large amount of toxic metals along with an explosive glass tube. Yet everyday we allow our children to spend hours watching it.

There are more than 500 man-made chemicals never before seen in our fatty tissues and in animals as well. This is happening all over the planet, even in Antarctica. These chemicals are accumulative and are something we won't be able to change within thousands of lifetimes. The unsuspecting consumer would no doubt be stunned to discover how many carcinogens are intertwined in our environment.

These hazardous materials disrupt the endocrine system and have adverse effects on every living thing on the planet. We cannot simply bury our trash in landfills. Companies that refuse to embrace green energy models are not saving money in the long run. They will have to pay for the damage caused by these products with liability claims. In order to save our species we all must vigilantly do our part. Corporations and business must adhere to some basic principles to keep our environment safe for the generations that will follow.

Some designers, such as the McDonough Braungart Design Chemistry are beginning to develop new products and architectural endeavors that embrace environmental health criteria. These pioneers are at the forefront of a new horizon. This new green engineering must become part of our future if we are to survive as a species.

The ideology of corporate greed and profits must change. Humans must use intelligence to design products and buildings that coexist with nature. We need to interact with the geochemistry of the Earth's surface and regenerate biological systems. We can do this by creating products that remember that our waste should equal food for other life forms. In nature, diversity works in concert with the sustainability of all organisms and if we cannot be flexible enough to change strategies when necessary, we may not be around to see the future.

Altering Lower Life Forms

"The life of the planet began the long, slow process of modulation an regulating the physical conditions of the planet. The oxygen in today's atmosphere is almost entirely the result of photosynthetic living, which had its start with the appearance of blue-green algae among the microorganisms."
--Lewis Thomas

Microorganisms remain one of the earliest signs of life on Earth. Microorganisms are very diverse and can be found in every part of the biosphere. They are in the soil, hot springs and on the ocean floor. They thrive deep inside rocks within the Earth's crust and high in our atmosphere. Microorganisms are a vital part of the nitrogen cycle and the ecosystem because these tiny creatures are responsible for the decomposing and recycling the soil.

In a single gram of fertile soil there can be over 100 million microorganisms. This includes bacteria, fungi protozoa, algae, earthworms, nematodes and insects. The relationship between these microorganisms is complex and somewhat difficult to decipher but we do know there is an ecological interdependence between these organisms. Together these microorganisms are responsible for the restructuring of organic material into fertile soil.

There is a strong possibility that genetically modified crops can cause our soil to become infertile and unusable. This ecological nightmare is worse than other forms of toxic waste and even nuclear pollution because after a period of time, these compounds break down. When genetically engineered plants lose their leave and seeds their DNA is left behind in the soil which leads to something called, "Horizontal gene transfer."

Horizontal gene transfer is the process in which an organism incorporates its genetic material to another organism without being the offspring of that organism. This could affect over 1,000 species of microorganisms. Genetic engineering is based on facilitating horizontal gene transfer between species, since they transfer material from animals to plants and vice versa.

The transfer of genetic material between species not only occurs naturally between bacteria and fungi but can also include higher organisms such as mammals. It isn't difficult to understand that this transfer of genetic material is only one hop away from man. It has already been suggested that this transferring process may have contributed to the emergence of new human pathogenic bacteria within the last 15 years.

To make matters worse, the DNA that is released from plants is not easily broken down. GM genes can survive for a long time, especially when adsorbed into solid particles such as sediment in the soil. The half-life of DNA (the time for half of the DNA to be broken down) in soil is 9.1 hours. In clay soil it takes 28.2 hours, which is more than enough time to transfer DNA to another organism. DNA is not only released when a cell dies but is actively secreted by living cells as well. It is through the uniting of these unrelated organisms that the diversity of the soil is being compromised.

Another problem is that GM seeds are designed to withstand high doses of pesticides and herbicides which buildup in the soil. Crops that contain built in pesticides such as Bt corn, loose their ability to ward off pests, as insects become immune to them. These extreme doses are harmful to soil insects that contribute to soil fertility.

Where ever genetically modified crops are planted again and again their DNA is being left behind and its' remnants are scattered for miles. The genetic material of GM crops has even been found where these crops were never planted. Genetic engineering is not the same as selective breeding and it doesn't take a rocket scientist to understand how this type of gene manipulation would never happen in nature.

Biological magnification refers to the process whereas certain substances such as pesticides or heavy metals move up the food chain but it can be used as an analogy for genetically modified DNA as well. The example of an anchovy that eats zoo-plankton containing a small amount of mercury can help give us a clear picture of what biological magnification is.

Over the lifetime of eating this plankton the anchovy has accumulated this mercury within its body. Tuna eat many anchovies over their life span. If the mercury has stunted the anchovy's growth, the anchovy will be smaller. That means the tuna must eat more anchovies to stay alive. In turn, more mercury is accumulating in the tuna. And so the chain of events continues. Biological magnification has occurred as the toxin is magnified in the tuna too. When we eat the tuna, we get the mercury that has been accumulating in these other species. The same processes occur on land as well.

Altering Humans

"The world as we have created it is a process of our thinking. It cannot be changed without changing our thinking."
--Albert Einstein

Within the Earth's various ecosystems, some of the smallest species make the biggest impact on recycling waste and pollution. Microorganisms do a wonderful job of restoring the natural balance but unfortunately, Homo sapiens are the most polluting species that Earth has ever seen. The pollution humans create may occurs at a different level but the implications affect every species, including us. Humans cannot quietly walk away from their pollution and leave it all up to microorganisms to sort out. We can't do that because there is simply too much of it. There's more fertilizer run off, toxic gases from factories, oil spills, and nuclear waste generated from nuclear reactors than the Earth can clean up.

In today's world nearly a billion people do not have access to clean, safe water. In the U.S. alone, farmers use more than 450 million kilograms of pesticides every year and have contaminated almost all of the nation's streams and rivers. As the population grows, so do the demands imposed on our ecosystem. Our natural resources are not invulnerable and infinitely available. Our society is beginning to become aware that the services our ecosystem provides for us are not only limited, but also threatened by human activities.

The term, ecosystems services are what biologists and economist are using for the many ways nature supports Earth's ecological health. The idea is not a new one, Plato understood that deforestation could lead to soil erosion. At that time, his observations and warnings went largely unnoticed. Since then many scientists and ecologists have been vehemently calling attention to these subtle and dangerous threats to human existence.

Societies are becoming aware of the problems that humans are creating within our ecosystem—even though nobody is willing to claim responsibility. Relatively new terminology is springing up in reference to the responsibility of restoration of the ecosystem.

The "Global Footprint" of business, corporations, and individuals may soon be assigned an economic value for the replacement costs of the ecosystem with anthropogenic alternatives. This may be the only way society can squelch the human greed factor. Evidently, we must address ecological issues by using the universal language that humans have learned to respond to—money. If that's what it takes to save the species, than that is what we must do. We must attach economic value to nature.

These ecological disasters need to stop and potential polluters should ask themselves if it's cheaper to fix what you've done or to do it right in the do it first place. It is up to governments to impose higher fines on those who kill our most valued assets. The higher the fine, the better, because loosing money is seemingly the only thing that influences corporate decision-making. Only if societies and governments stand firm, punishing acts against nature, will there be a discernable difference in business practices. The question is, will it be too little, too late. Meanwhile, the drum keeps banging louder every day, as humans inhabit new geographical areas and become susceptible to new diseases that are crossing the boarders of species.

Diseases Crossing the Barrier of Species

"There's no one place a virus goes to die—but that doesn't make its demise any less a public health victory. Throughout human history, viral diseases have had their way with us, and for just as long, we have hunted them down and done our best to wipe the out."
--Jeffrey Kluger

One of the most cataclysmic disasters that can bring a civilization to its knees is a pandemic of global proportions. During the 14th century, the Bubonic Plague or Black Death left a trail of corpses piled in the streets from Europe to Egypt and also across Asia. It was an excruciating, painful death. About 75 million people died at a time when there were only about 360 million people around the area to begin with. A bacterial disease that is carried by rodents causes the plague. It became deadly when it crossed the barrier of species to humans.

Humans have evolved and so have viruses. Humans are not being threatened by new viral species but by animal viruses that have gained the ability, throughout the passing of decades, to switch hosts—infecting the human population. Although the process of switching hosts involves many factors, including intrinsic characteristics of the viruses, environmental factors, demographic and cellular barriers, there is some predictability of which viruses may successfully cross the barrier of species.

Zoonoses or zoonose are infectious diseases that can be transmitted from non-human animals (both wild and domesticated) to humans. Of the 1415 known pathogens that affect humans, 61% are zoonotic in nature. Some of the most feared threats around the world are diseases such as: Ebola, SARS, Encephalitis, H1N1, Swine Flu, Bird Flu, Rabies, Monkeypox, Malaria and West Nile virus. You don't have to travel to the jungle or the rainforest to find animals vectors that can carry or spread these diseases. Animals that have been known to have diseases that crossed the barrier to humans surround us. Some of them include dogs, cats, birds, ferrets, fish, horses, reptiles, livestock and petting zoo animals. Rover or Fluffy may not be infected but when left outside to explore, they could easily come in contact with a disease such as rabies.

Still, many researchers now believe that the increasing likelihood of these types of bacterial and viral diseases is the result of the Earth's depleting ecosystems. According to a report in the Journal of Conservation Biology, it is estimated that nearly one quarter of the world's plants and vertebrate animal species could be extinct by 2050 due of habitat changes brought on by human urbanization. Diseases that jump the species barrier to humans have been traced to human interaction, increased exposure and close contact with animals. As food supplies diminish, meat hunters forage for bush meat. Humans are continuously in close contact with primates and other animals. With food prices rising, people are unable to afford the basics in places like central Africa. They are increasingly turning to the forests for food, while exposing themselves to hidden dangers.

Many modern diseases and epidemic diseases start out as zoonotic diseases. There is good evidence that measles, influenza, smallpox, diphtheria and HIV came to humans in this way. Even the common cold and tuberculosis may have begun in other species. Salmonella and Lyme disease are zoonotic diseases.

Animals with high mobility such as birds and bats present a greater risk of zoonotic transmission because they can easily move into areas that humans inhabit. Public health officials predict that animal diseases will cross the species barrier faster than ever in recorded history due to this close interaction.

Some zoonotic diseases are transmitted directly from infected animals to people, while others require a vector such as a tick of a mosquito to be spread. Although diseases that are transmitted through vectors pose a particular threat in continents such as: Africa, Asia and South America, the good news is by controlling the population of mosquitoes and other vectors, disease can also be controlled to some extent.

What are the odds of more viruses crossing the boundaries of the species and starting a devastating pandemic? Unfortunately, it's very likely that a serious pandemic will happen within the next 50 years. If that were to occur, it is estimated that 1 billion people would be sickened and approximately 165 million would die. With our increasing global population, our only hope may be in detecting and catching these zoonotic diseases in their infancy. In order for public health officials to get a handle on these diseases it will require international cooperation. Even with that, it will be difficult to predict which diseases will cross the barriers between species.

As frightening as a pandemic sounds, if an outbreak were to occur, it probably wouldn't lead to the demise of Homo sapiens.

However, humans already have many factors working against sustainable life and a global pandemic wouldn't help matters. The next serious threat for extinction is born through human technology. It begins a new chapter of a changing landscape that is almost invisible to the naked eye, yet could have serious consequences for our species.

Electric Power Fields

"Invention is the most important product of man's creative brain. The ultimate purpose is the complete mastery of mind over the material world, the harnessing of human nature to human needs."
--Nikola Tesla, *My Inventions*

The utilization of electric and magnet fields have catapulted humans into the technology world and beyond. But as these new technologies unfold, we are becoming aware of some very troubling ramifications. We are traveling down this technological road at an exponential rate. Where is it taking us, and is this trail really safe to travel?

The initials EMF stand for electric magnetic field. It refers to something that is invisible to the human eye, yet invariably surrounds us. They form the invisible lines of force that surround any electrical device that is plugged in and turned on. Electric fields produce electric charges and magnetic fields. That flow of current goes through the wires or electrical devices we have around our homes and offices. EMFs are also associated with power lines and mobile phone masts. The sensation caused by strong electric fields resonating from high-voltage electricity has many people concerned about its potential health consequences. The International Agency for Research on Cancer and the National Institute of Environmental Health Sciences (NIEHS) both found that power line and magnetic fields are a possible cause of cancer. Yet, in the United States there are no federal standards that limit occupational or residential exposure to these power lines.

These fields can and do cause diseases and health problems by the "smog" they produce. It has been only within the last couple of decades that research into how these power fields affect the health of humans and other species has come into question. New evidence is revealing that cell phone towers and mobile phone masts are disorienting the great pollinators of the planet. With the loss of pollinators, humans have little chance of survival because we adapted as hunters and gathers first. Additionally, the compounding frequency of exposure to power fields is contributing to an alarming number of sensitivities, along with possibly changing the human normal biorhythms.

Most of us never give power fields a thought. As consumers we just accept that new innovations are harmless. Power fields have become so prevalent in our society that we don't perceive any danger. The World Health Organization, (WHO) considers electric smog to be, "one of the most common and fastest growing environmental influences," and too much exposure to it can cause illness and premature death.

Electric fields are one of the three types of fields. The electric field is the field composed of the wires around your house or office and is turned on at all times whether electric is being used or not.

The second type of field is called magnetic. This type of field is the sum of appliances such as electric blankets, toasters, hair dryers, shavers and clock radios, to name a few. Magnetic fields do rapidly decrease their intensity with distance but the danger lies in their close use to the body. For example, an electric blanket is used directly on the body and operates all night while someone is sleeping. This accumulation of exposure to magnetic fields over a period of time is suspected of throwing off the body's natural current.

The third type of field is called a radio frequency field. Components of this field are televisions, microwave ovens, radio transmitters, cell phones and mobile phone masts. The frequent use of cell phones and their proximity to the head, has become a public health concern of late.

Tiny particles of energy are given off from a variety of household items, including computers. They are in the air we breathe. The international Agency for Research on Cancer has called electric smog, a carcinogen. A study conducted by the National Radiological Protection Board concluded that children have doubled their risk of leukemia when they are exposed to high levels of electromagnetic radiation.

Power field can be found all over the globe with more being erected perpetually. Scientists now estimate that our exposure to EMF's and their smog is 100 million times higher than it was in our grandparent's days. It is also expected that levels will continue to increase as technology advances.

All the toys and gadgets humans build are creating a web of fields that are wreaking havoc between natural basic underlying systems. Not only is the human biorhythm being altered but also we are gradually changing the health of other species. About the only thing humans can do to reduce the risk of these field is by reducing exposure and limiting the time spent near EMFs. As more cell phone towers continue to populate the landscape, the less likely that is to happen. Humans are altering the planet with their technology and in doing so they are taking out species that effects our own fragile existence. Our technology is an insidious cloud over our heads that keeps growing. Will the inventions of our boundless technology force us forever into oblivion?

The Demise of the Pollinators

"If the bee disappears from the surface of the Earth, man would have no more than four years to live. No more bees, no more pollination, no more man."
--Albert Einstein

Einstein's statement about bees came long before the mystery of colony collapse disorder had been observed but his words should serve as a warning of a world void of bees and thus the extinction of prime pollinators. Without them our world will become an artificial zoo of fake foods with properties that breech natures' boundaries. Fruits and vegetables will be difficult to be found and we will have to depend on science to fabricate new inventions that can pass for food.

Gradually, man is changing the Earth and not for the better. Bees and other pollinating creatures are merely a sensitive barometer of the horrific influences of our industrial society. The phenomenon called 'colony collapse disorder' is the name given to the drastic disappearance of the Western honey bee colonies. Beekeepers everywhere are waking up to the bewildering surprise of only a queen and a few immature workers in hives that were filled with bees only the day before. No dead bees to be found around the area. The bees are just simply disappearing. What is left of the hive will not survive and beekeepers have few clues as to the causes.

Colony collapse disorder was first noticed in 2006 in North America, when a significant amount of bees began disappearing from beekeepers' hives. Meanwhile, beekeepers in Europe were also observing the same disastrous phenomena. It was happening all over Europe. The initial reports coming in from Switzerland and Germany represented declines of greater than 50% of their hives. Other beekeepers also began noticing declines in Belgium, Greece, Italy, Portugal, France, Spain and the Netherlands. Soon a frantic investigation of the disappearing bees was underway.

Fast-forwarding to today, when there is still no definite answer for the diminishing numbers of honeybees. Some authorities have attributed the problem to mites and insect infestation within the hives, while other explanations range from disorientation from cell phone towers to genetically modified crops and pesticides lowering the bee's resistance. In truth, colony collapse disorder may have several contributing factors.

Farms grow crops in huge blocks, producing one single crop such as corn. Bees are transported in trucks to these farms, as this is the usual practice in migratory bee keeping. They are then hoisted away to another such farm, while the queen is often artificially inseminated to genetically alter her reproduction. Some researchers have attributed bee loses with the feeding of high-fructose corn syrup as attempt to supplement winter storage. Still other researchers fear that effects of genetically modified crops are playing a major role in the loss of bees everywhere. These crops, are heavily doused with insecticides and herbicides, and there is evidence that this material lay dormant inside the bees. Insecticides and herbicides have been found in the hives and the honey that bees produce. The Organic Consumers Association reported that colony collapse disorder was not occurring at organic bee keeping operations.

A recent report from the USDA states that a high number of viruses and other pathogens, pesticides and parasites were present in colony collapse disorder colonies. It is now suggested that a combination of environmental stresses might be setting off a cascade of events that is weakening the bees. This makes them more susceptible to pests and pathogens in general.

There may be more than one reason why bees are disappearing but some scientists believe bees have a distinct sensitivity to electric fields because they carry an electrical charge naturally. This electric charge helps bees find their hives. Electric fields might not be the sole cause of colony collapse disorder but it is certainly a probable factor.

How serious would the outcome be if bees disappeared from the face of the Earth? The four most common species of bees in the U.S. has dropped by 95% in the past few decades. Scientists state, that if this trend continues it will have devastating implications. Because bees pollinate some 90% of the worlds' commercial plants including most fruits, vegetables and nuts, life without them would be hard to imagine.

Without pollinators there wouldn't be any coffee, Soya beans or cotton. That would change the needs for other products that would otherwise seem unrelated to food. Still, our food sources would sharply dwindle. The food chain for humans depends on the pollinators. Not only bees but also other crucial pollinators such as the moth and hoverflies have also been in decline over the past few decades. It is clear that something is changing within the world of insects. Loosing the pollinators will change life on Earth for humans and every other species because we are all connected within this ecosystem. Try to imagine a world without the foods we presently enjoy. Without the pollinators, humans would most assuredly starve.

Have we already reached the tipping point on the amount of EMFs in our atmosphere? Could the sensitive of the bees be yet another warning of what's to come? Put into perspective, the decline of the pollinators is just one more obstacle that Homo sapiens will have to conquer if we want to avoid extinction.

Electro Sensitivity in Man

"In a world where a drug cannot be launched without proof that it is safe, where the use of herbs and natural compounds available to all since early Egyptian times are now questioned, their safety subjected to the deepest scrutiny, where a new food cannot be launched without prior approval, the idea that we can use mobile telephone, including masts, and introduce WiFi and mobile phones without restrictions around our 5 year olds is double-standards gone mad. I speak, not just as an editor and scientist that has looked in depth at all the research but as a father that lost his beloved daughter to a brain tumor."
--Chris Woolham M.A., Biochemistry (Oxon)

Yes, electromagnetic fields are all around us. These electromagnetic fields can produce a form of radiation that is called electromagnetic radiation. It doesn't matter where you live; they emanate from power lines, televisions and household electrical wiring. These fields bombard us whenever we talk on the phone, use the microwave or take advantage of our wireless Internet connection. During the last couple of decades, the populations of developed countries have experienced serious electrohypersensitivity to these fields. It has been estimated that 3-8% of the population develops serious symptoms from EMF's, while some 35% experience milder symptoms.

Symptoms of human sensitivity to EMFs may include nausea, dizziness, headaches, fatigue, depression, and sleep disturbances when becoming 'allergic' to electricity. In severe cases, lifestyle changes are necessary. These changes in lifestyle should include; unplugging electrical appliances when not in use, limiting electric appliances throughout the home, especially appliances that are within close proximity to the head.

Other lifestyle change would be to replace florescent lights with natural incandescent bulbs or candlelight. One of the latest inventions is the new compact fluorescent bulb (CFL), which is being pushed on the public as energy savers. These new bulbs can interfere with radios, cordless phones, and remote controls. They have trigger migraine headaches, skin irritations and other symptoms in Electro sensitive individuals.

Further investigation of this new curly, bulb reveals that they emit high levels of ultraviolet radiation—specifically, UVC and UVA rays. The UV rays are so strong they can actually burn the skin. Some experts say this radiation could even initiate cell death and cause the deadliest form of skin cancer—melanoma. Researchers that have tested these bulbs found that the protective phosphor coating of the light bulb was cracked in every bulb that was tested. The cracks allowed their dangerous UV rays to escape into the atmosphere. The manufacturers of these bulbs 'suggest' users avoid close contact and limiting the duration to one hour a day. Bulbs that contain mercury inside of them also require 'special disposal' in a toxic waste depot, rather than being tossed out with the regular household trash.

If that isn't serious enough, if you accidentally break one of these bulbs it will release mercury vapor into the air. The Institute for Molecular and Nanoscale Innovation measured the mercury vapors of a broken bulb to be as high as, 800 mcg/m3, which is eight times higher than the occupational exposure limit for a workers eight-hour day. If a child were exposed to the mercury vapor from a broken CFL bulb they would be subjected to eight thousand times more than the recommended limit.

Broken CFL bulb releases 30% of its mercury over a four-day period, the rest of the mercury remains trapped in the bulb. This adheres to another major problem—more toxic waste materials to be housed somewhere on planet Earth. According to the King County Hazardous Waste Program, crushing and breaking fluorescent lamps release mercury vapor and mercury-containing phosphor powder. These substances can be difficult to contain. Unfortunately, CFL bulbs would amount to, just more hazardous material left to seep into the ground water. This is something we have plenty of already.

Clean up involves closing off the room where the broken bulb is and calling in a HazMat team. As frightening as that sounds it tends to be quite costly as well. There is some research being done on a cloth made with the nanomaterial (nanoselim) which claims to be capable of capturing mercury emissions for proper disposal. If and when such cloths were available commercially to the public, how would we dispose of them?

With all the dangerous fields around us already, you might think technology would generate new products that didn't spawn more environmental threats. However, new and threatening products abound constantly, testing our limits and vulnerabilities. This is a system that allows new advancements to slip through the cracks and go unchecked until they are proven to have devastating effects. They leave the human consumer largely in the dark as to their pernicious nature. Anyone, who chooses to be mindful of health issues, should take precautions and minimize the time spent around EMFs.

Another thing to keep in mind is that metal frame beds and waterbeds attract EMFs. Since the radiation from electromagnetic fields is accumulative, it is imperative that we reduce our exposure to it. Some simple solutions would be to replace metal frame beds with wood frame beds or Futon type frames. Move beds and cribs a few feet away from walls with electrical wires and avoid the placement of beds on the wall opposite of computers, televisions, microwaves and clothes dryers. Most walls do not block the magnetic fields of electrical appliances.

Regardless of whether you are sensitive to EMFs, everyone should protect himself or herself. Minimize computer use and cell phone use. Keep laptops off the lap and away from metal surfaces. If at all possible, avoid installing wireless networks. Don't purchase a DECT cordless phone, they transmit a strong RF signal, even when sitting in it's cradle. Also, unplug cordless phones at night or store them in another room.

Cell phones are particularly dangerous for children because their skull is thinner and still developing. Children under the age of 16 should not use cell phones, unless there is an emergency. Everyone should avoid playing games or watching movies on cell phones. It is also important to avoid using cell phones in cars, trains, subways and planes. Radiation gets trapped in closed metal zones. And never keep cell phones in your purse, pocket or near the back or hip area. The hip area produces 80% of all red blood cells and is especially venerable to EMR damage.

Keeping electromagnetic fields away from the body is very important. Try to eliminate the use of electric blankets and electric heating pads. Remember that the exposure you get is not only accumulative over time but is more intense the closer the devices are to the body. Even when cooking on electric stoves, use the back burners as much as possible. When using the microwave oven, stand at least 5 feet away when it is operational. If you're concerned about electric smog exposure, you may want to purchase an electric smog detector to determine if you have any leaks from microwaves or other devices.

People who suffer from hypersensitivity to electromagnetic fields may not be within the majority of the population but there is compelling evidence that what has been affecting insects and other species, is also affecting humans. Still, since hypersensitivity issues began to arise, the makers of these devices swear by their safety. Of course, if you were in the cell-phone business it would be hard to admit that the products you were manufacturing was the cause of brain cancer. Instead you might look for any other possible cause.

Ever since health issues and hypersensitivity brought about some legal suits against cell phone makers, they have fought back, tooth and nail. The industry wanted to paint the picture that those who suffer from hypersensitivity to electromagnetic fields, were hypochondriacs or kooks. For the most part, hypersensitivity could be difficult to diagnose as such, since the symptoms may vary between individuals. The one thing that is perfectly clear is that what humans are inventing with new technologies is harmful in the long run.

EMFs are disrupting the migratory patterns of insects, birds and the biorhythms of humans. Electromagnetic fields are revamping our physical world. They are another link in the chain of destructive behaviors that humans have taken on—which has the ability to finish us off. That is the problem for a technologically advanced society. It happens when scrutiny of safety issues is the last consideration. Humans have created many things that have later been found to be harmful. The menacing health risks of EMFs are indeed perilous but they are nothing, when compared to the most deadly invention man has stumbled upon; which is nuclear energy.

Nuclear Power and Nuclear Waste

"There are two problems for our species' survival—nuclear war and environmental catastrophe—and we're hurling towards them. Knowingly."
--Noam Chomsky

The birth of the nuclear age was only beginning in 1939, when Albert Einstein and several other scientists wrote to then President Franklin D. Roosevelt to warn of Nazi Germanys' efforts to purify uranium-235, which could be used to build an atomic bomb. Shortly after that the United States Government initiated the Manhattan Project.

Over the next six years, more than $2 billion was spent to create the formulas for refining uranium and putting together the atomic bomb. Although Einstein didn't work on the bomb directly, it was due to his equation, ($E = mc^2$) and action that led to the U.S. concern to create the atomic bomb. Albert Einstein must have realized the horrendous implications of atomic energy when he told *Newsweek*, "Had I known that the Germans would not succeed in producing an atomic bomb, I never would have lifted a finger."

Since the first atomic bomb, nuclear energy was proliferated as a revelation from the fossil fuel dilemma. It has been promoted to public as a safe, clean energy source when it is neither of those things. It is not safe because radioactivity is innately dangerous to all living things and one small accident—whether it's due to a miscalculation by man or an act of nature—can have catastrophic results. Nuclear energy is not clean either because of the waste material it leaves behind to be stored. That can range anywhere from a few days for very short-lived isotopes to millions of years for spent nuclear fuel.

According to the U.S. Government Accounting Office, spent nuclear power fuel is "Considered one of the most hazardous substances on Earth." Yet, the U.S. Nuclear Regulatory Commission permits U.S. spent reactor fuel pools to hold, on the average, 4-5 times the amount that the Fukushima reactors stored. Since the early 1980's the U.S. has been allowed to store nuclear spent fuel in high density storage with the expectation that the U.S. Government would open a permanent depository for spent fuel waste.

Essentially, the U.S. Government is storing 4-5 times more spent fuel than they were designed to hold in these reactor fuel pools. These pools were originally meant to be temporary storage for a period of only 5 years. Since they were intended to be only temporary they were not required to have in-depth nuclear safety requirements.

Just like the Fukushima reactors, the U.S. spent fuel pools are located outside of the containment structure. But they don't have secondary containment areas or a redundant power source. Some of these buildings even have tin roofs and resemble a more casual structure such as a car dealership or a Wal-Mart. These structures that house spent nuclear fuel pools, for all appearances, don't feel like the potential national threat that they are. How easy would it be for a terrorist group to invade or destroy any of these structures? This is a subject that few would choose to discuss.

The National Research Counsel released its findings regarding the vulnerabilities of these spent fuel pools as, "A loss-of-pool-coolant event resulting from damage or collapse of the pool could have severe consequences. It is not prudent to dismiss nuclear plants, including spent fuel storage facilities as undesirable targets for terrorists."

As of January 2013, there were 31 countries that had nuclear power plants worldwide. Altogether the total amount of nuclear power plants worldwide is 437; another 68 new nuclear power plants are currently under construction. It has only been since the Fukushima accident that the Nuclear Regulatory Commission got around to requiring operators to have instrumentation in control rooms to tell them, water levels, water chemistry and the water temperature of these pools. This is particularly frightening because the rupture of nuclear fluid rods releases most of the cesium-137 abundant long-lived radionuclides. A natural disaster such as an earthquake can easily set off another cataclysmic event that would need to be addressed immediately.

Cesium-137 has a 30-year half-life and persists in the ecosystem for 180-300 years. It is water-soluble and easily becomes ubiquitous within the ecosystem. Its macronutrients even mimic potassium. But soil contamination is hardly the only concern here. Any nuclear accident that causes fuel rods to rupture or melt will cause a release of cesium gas. As seen in the Chernobyl accident, the winds were blowing to the Northwest leaving dire consequences for another country, Scandinavia.

The Chernobyl accident is considered the most serious nuclear accident in the history of nuclear energy. The explosion that occurred in one of the reactors prompted fires that lasted for 10 days and led to huge amounts of radioactive materials being released into the environment. A cloud of radioactive material spread over much of Europe, with the greatest contamination around the reactor area.

Since the Chernobyl accident, congenital birth defects have increased by 250%. It is estimated that more than 5 million people were 'contaminated' with radioactive materials from the Chernobyl accident. Children born in Scandinavia at the time of the accident were born intellectually impaired largely because the food the mother ingested was also contaminated and was taken in by the embryo. Damage to the genes of the unborn altered all parts of their bodies.

Studies of areas affected reveals that after 27 years, high levels of contamination still linger in many places. Toxicology reports indicate that everything in the environment was affected from viruses, birds, plants, bacteria, trees and cows. These changes are still apparent even today.

In Gomel, which is less than 50 miles away from Chernobyl, cesium contamination levels are 40 times higher than the recognized danger level. Sadly, an untold number of people will continue to die from cancers and other diseases caused by the Chernobyl accident. Chernobyl should have been the world's last nuclear accident but because Homo sapiens evidently, don't learn quickly, we got another lesson when Japan suffered an earthquake, tsunami, and the nuclear disaster at Fukushima.

Naoto Kan was Prime Minister of Japan when Fukushima disaster occurred in 2011. He was recently quoted as saying, "My conclusions is that the safest nuclear power plant means not having nuclear power plants at all." He recalls how after 8 hours of earthquakes, the reactors and spent fuel pools almost went completely out of control. That was when the TEPCO requested withdrawal of their workers. If he had allowed that to happen, it would have been almost impossible to keep the nuclear ration under control. But it is still not under total control. Tokyo is almost 200 miles from Fukushima yet soil samples taken from various areas qualify as nuclear waste and would have to be contained in a nuclear disposal site in the U.S. if the accident had happened here.

The Fukushima plant itself is by no means contained either. It has been over two and a half years since the Fukushima disaster began but the plant still continues to store more than 90 million gallons of radioactive water. As troubling as that is, the most abhorrent reality is that the plant is and has been leaking 400 tons of toxic water daily, into the Pacific Ocean. Almost weekly plant operators acknowledge a new leak. Proposed solutions for the problem, is at best, 'something to try.' This ecological nightmare is a

46

slow-burning environmental disaster with uncharted implications for sea life, wildlife and up the food chain to us.

As this radioactive wastewater pours into the Pacific Ocean it reaches other shores. It flows northward to Alaska then down the coast of Canada and the Western coast of the United States. Both cesium-137 and strontium-90 have a half-life of about 30 years but it takes 10 half-lives for these isotopes to decay down to nothing. Meanwhile, the plankton in the Pacific Ocean is being contaminated. As the contamination is spread up the food chain it continues to grow in concentration as well. Shrimp, fish and oysters eat plankton and therefore, the more they eat, the more that radiation will be concentrated as it makes it way up the food chain. We must remember that radionuclides are lethal at the atomic level and that everything they touch threatens life of every form.

Do governments that have active nuclear power plants realize the catastrophic dangers they are subjecting us to? If human error was never a consideration or possibility, there still would be plenty of probable natural disasters that could start a chain reaction. The safety of containing nuclear power plants and spent fuel pools would come down to a flip of the coincidental coin. Radioactive nuclides may be something new to us as a species but they are millions of times more poisonous than any other poison that we are familiar with. They cause cancer, leukemia, genetic mutations, birth defects, and malformations all while remaining invisible to our senses.

At least one government official has been astute enough to comprehend the big picture here. Germany has announced that it plans to abandon all nuclear energy by 2022. In a statement, Chancellor Angela Merkel said, "We believe that we can show those countries who decide to abandon nuclear power or not to start using it, how it is possible to achieve growth, creating jobs and economic prosperity while shifting the energy supply toward renewable energies." Merkel, who holds a Ph.D. in physics had initially pushed through a plan to extend the life of some of the country's reactors but changed her mind due to the catastrophe at Japan's Fukushima Dai-ichi nuclear plant. The disaster must have made her rethink the technology's risks.

In the United States, nuclear power reactor manufacturer, General Electric is spinning the media to avoid public alarm. The nuclear power industry insists that nuclear power is still safe. Public officials including President Obama, advise the public not to worry and that no preparations are necessary. They will let us know if we need to be aware of anything.

The fact is that radiation leaking from the Fukushima plant is presently at higher levels now, than it has been within the last 2 years.

Still there is no end in sight and governments seem adamant to temp Murphy's law again. Nuclear power and all its waste lay waiting for another chance to annihilate us. They are one more menacing storm in the distance that is approaching with inevitable speed.

It won't matter if some countries disable their nuclear power plants. It won't even matter if Japan can somehow stop leaking radioactive material into the Pacific Ocean. Because a world that soon will contains over 500 nuclear power plants will be doing more than just temping fate. Especially when you consider that our planet is getting hotter and extremes in weather along with forceful storms will be imminent.

The only way we can ever be safe from the dangers of nuclear power is if all counties stop using it. This would require the various governments of the world to cooperate with each other and recognize the dire consequences of nuclear energy. If that type of cooperation is possible we may be well on our way to saving our species. If we as a species can finally make use of our evolved intellect, we may stand a chance to face off with some external causes of extinction. One of the fiercest extra-terrestrial forces coming our way is the asteroid.

Asteroids, Comets, Meteors and Space Trash

"Since, in the long run, every planetary civilization will be endangered by impacts from space, every surviving civilization is obliged to become space-faring—not because of exploratory or romantic zeal, but for the most practical reason imaginable: staying alive. If our long-term survival is at stake, we have a basic responsibility to our species to venture to other worlds."
--Carl Sagan

An asteroid is generally believed to have triggered one of the worst mass extinction events in history, taking out the dinosaurs and many other species, in its wake. They are minor planets. They are shattered remnants of planetesimals that never grew large enough to become planets. They are leftovers from the formation of our solar system. There are millions of asteroids that orbit the Earth within the asteroid belt. There are also many asteroids that lie outside of the main asteroid belt as well. If you took all the asteroids that exist, the total mass would be less than that of the Earth's moon. Scientists estimate there are more than 750,000 asteroids that are larger than three-fifths of a mile within the asteroid belt. Some asteroids might only be the size of a small car or a building but despite their size, if they crash into our planet they can do a lot of damage.

Earth has and will continue to be hit with asteroids. We're not always aware of many asteroid hit the Earth because they often fall into the ocean. If an asteroid would hit Earth it would have to be more than a quarter-mile wide to be capable of a global disaster. If such an asteroid were to hit Earth, it would raise enough dust in our atmosphere to cause a "nuclear winter".

On February 15, 2012 an asteroid was expected to barely miss hitting Earth at 24, 00 km. The asteroid passed the Earth closer than many commercial satellites, making it possible to be visible with a pair of household binoculars. While the asteroid had not been expected to impact Earth, the 164-foot space rock only narrowly missed us. Even smaller asteroids, which are believed to strike Earth every 1,000 to 10,000 years, could destroy a city or cause devastating tsunamis when plunged into the ocean. Scientist warn that there could be as many as 500,000 objects measuring to 98 feet that are still undiscovered.

While there are dozens of asteroids that have been classified as "potentially hazardous" by the scientists who track them, many others could potentially be sent on a collision course with Earth if their orbit became 'perturbed' in the distant future. The perturbation is a slight departure from the closed elliptical orbit that slowly changes planetary orbits. Theoretical physicist Dr. Michio Kaku, believes even small asteroids such as the one that recently exploded over Russia can cause quite a disaster. That asteroid caused thousand of injuries just from the shockwaves that blew out windows and shook buildings. Kaku points out, that so far the asteroids we've encountered have been "city-busters," but in 2036 we will have a "nation-buster." According to Kaku, the asteroid Apophis, will graze Earth's atmosphere in 2029 and depending on how much friction is created during its flyby, it could hit us on its next pass in 2036.

Kaku doesn't seem worried though. He says some dramatic plans are being devised to deal with asteroids. A rocket could be strategically placed to nudge the asteroid 'slightly out of the way' just in the nick of time and could save the day. So when Apophis makes that second pass of it will just miss the Earth.

Astronomers are also watching the skies for comets. While scientists are unsure if comets or minor planets will actually hit us, they estimate an explosion of that magnitude would be 50 times greater that the biggest nuclear bomb that has ever been detonated.

The comet ISON dubbed the "comet of the century" by NASA will make its closest approach to the Sun in late November. If the comet survives it could emerge glowing as bright as the moon and its debris will travel to Earth. Scientist say that we will notice blue noctilucent clouds, as the dust from the comet eventually falls to Earth. Over several years the dust would dissipate and slowly filter out of the atmosphere.

Meteors are another possible catastrophic event waiting in the wings. Until recently, NASA has only been looking for space rocks that were 100 feet wide and bigger. Previously, it had been estimated that there were about 3 million space rocks out there about that size but now it's known there are about 20 million of them out there.

The asteroid defection exercise is a good idea. It would no doubt be effective for nudging smaller asteroids and even the space junk that we ourselves put out there. On September 23, (a day earlier than expected) NASA was expecting 26 large pieces of a bus sized satellite to survive the re-entry of the Earth's surface. The debris was expected to fall over a 500-mile long area but with only a 1-in-3200 chance of hitting a person on the ground. The spent satellite is only one of some 22,000 dead or dying satellites and other debris that orbits the earth. Out of that number, about one object re-enters Earth's atmosphere a day. To be sure, many people have been hit by junk falling from the sky. On average, about 1,000 people a year are hit by falling debris. The National Research Council warns that soon there will be too much space trash for satellites or space stations to safely stay in orbit. It means future generations will have a heck of a lot of debris to nudge off course or dispose of.

Whether the threat is from a asteroid, comet, meteor or our own space trash coming back to haunt us, we need to know where it is and when it's on its way to Earth. One bright spot in the search and tracking of asteroids comes in the form of a new space telescope. The anticipated launch of Sentinel, in 2018 will orbit around the sun in order to give us a better view.

The trajectory of space rocks can typically be determined with some reliability. Even though the path of these objects may change in the future, if they can be observed early enough we should have time to act. The hard part is in locating them in time to stop a direct hit. If we can see them coming we may be able to avoid the fate of the dinosaurs.

Will our intelligence enable us to divert the paths of these extra-terrestrial space objects? Homo sapiens could conquer asteroids and the like but what about the extra-terrestrial types whom don't land here with a thump? Should we be afraid that Earth could be visited from aliens who would decide to take over the planet?

Extra-terrestrials

"Given the millions of billions of Earth-like planets, life elsewhere in the Universe without a doubt, does exist. In the vastness of the Universe we are not alone."
--Albert Einstein The Bible According to Albert Einstein

On November 16, 1974 a message was broadcast into the outer space through frequency modulated radio waves. This message was intended to communicate with aliens if there were any out there. From the Arecibo radio telescope in Puerto Rico the message was sent in binary code and figures. It consisted of 1679 binary digits, approximately 210 bytes and was created by Dr. Frank Drake and Dr. Carl Sagan. The message contained a graphic that presented key factors about humans and the planet Earth. It was intended to reach out into the depths of space to locate any advanced civilizations and to distinguish humans as a friendly, welcoming species.

About 27 years later an almost identical pattern appeared in the form of a crop circle that was right in front of a similar radio telescope. The reply message in the crop circle, although similar within the calculation system, except that this drawing was of humanoid with a large head and it indicated that silica was the dominant in its life forms instead of carbon. Within the message, it was also explained that they were inhabitants of the 3rd, 4th, and 5th planets of their solar system who also have an extra string within their DNA.

The following year another picture appeared in the form of a crop circle in Crabwood, with a face that was unmistakable extra-terrestrial. There was something else within the picture. It appeared to be a CD with a coded message. Data expert, Paul Vigay managed to decipher that message.

The Message:

Beware of bearers of false gifts and their broken promises
Much pain but still time
There is good out there

We oppose deception
Conduit closing

The National UFO Reporting Center (NUFORC) keeps records of worldwide sightings of UFO's. Prior to 2012, the world sightings of UFO have averaged around 4500 per year. Then in 2012 the number of worldwide sightings spiked to 7914. In 2013 the worldwide UFO sightings topped 7478. Thousands of people around the world have reported UFO sightings. There have been hundreds of photos of UFO's and even videos to prove that aliens really exist, have visited and are still visiting us.

Archaeologists have found ancient ruins and depictions of aliens as gods. There are pictures of flying saucers and stars as well as aliens drawn on cave walls all around the world. Is this proof that aliens have visited Earth in the past? Many proponents point to physical evidence such as the pyramids, stone drawings, stone sculptures and religious text as proof that we have been visited in the past.

The Sanskrit epics that were written in India more than two millennia ago make reference to mythical flying machines. There are lines etched in high plateaus in the Peruvian desert that have baffled archaeologists for decades. Giant carved blocks with such precise workmanship that even with today's modern tools would be nearly impossible to replicate. How could people from these early civilizations have managed to erect these structures without help? Have ancient aliens landed on Earth to somehow shape our civilization?

World-renowned scientist, Stephen Hawking believes extra-terrestrial life almost certainly exists, and that humans should be extremely cautious about interacting with them. Hawkins says, "We only have to look at ourselves to see how intelligent life might develop into something we wouldn't want to meet. I imagine they might exist in massive ships, having used up all the resources from their home planet. Such advanced aliens would perhaps become nomads, looking to conquer and colonize whatever planets the can reach."

Some highly educated people believe aliens have visited us for a very long time. Stanton Friedman, who has a Master's degree in nuclear physics and worked on fusion and fission rockets for decades, is one of them. Friedman spent half of the last half-century researching UFO's and recently told the world what he uncovered. "Some UFO's are intelligently controlled extra-terrestrial spacecraft, and this is the biggest story of the millennium. I'm convinced we're dealing here with a cosmic Watergate." Friedman also told AOL News that, "A few people within major governments have known since at least 1947 that some UFO's are alien spacecraft." Friedman says high-ranking officials have carefully covered up all the hard evidence of UFO's and that many scientists are afraid to expose the truth. Former astronaut, Edgar Mitchell shares Friedman's views and believes that in 1947 in Roswell, New Mexico there was an alien spacecraft crash.

World governments, in an effort to ward off mass hysteria, deny the existence of UFO's and try to explain these sightings as natural phenomenon. However, with all the continuous evidence coming in, alien visitation is hard to deny. Ancient societies have recorded sightings of aliens worldwide yet they did not seem fearful of them; instead they considered them Gods. If aliens have visited Earth for thousands of years, they would have already had many opportunities to conquer Earth

Carl Sagan once asked the question, "What does it mean for a civilization to be a million years old? We have had radio telescopes and spaceships for a few decades; our technical civilization is a few hundred years old, an advanced civilization millions of years old is as much beyond us as we are beyond a bush baby or a macaque." Indeed, any alien civilization that had the ability to visit Earth for thousands of years must be extremely more advanced than ours.

Michio Kaku, professor of theoretical physics at City University of New York, defines an alien civilization that is advanced enough to visit Earth as a Type 111 civilization. A type 1 civilization delineates a technological level similar to ours at the present time. Type 11 civilizations would be capable of harnessing the energy of their own star, something humans are on the verge of aspiring to. But a type 111 civilization would have the ability to harness and utilize the energy of their own galaxy. Any extra-terrestrial beings visiting Earth would have knowledge of how to travel through wormholes to quickly tunnel space-time bridging two universes. They would make use of wormhole vortexes here on Earth. Such a highly evolved civilization could have easily taken us out at any time if they had desired to do that.

Some believe there are twelve portals that alien civilization use here on Earth, the most famous of these is the Bermuda Triangle. The portal system forms two lines around the globe, with two others at the North and South poles. These portals or wormholes connect planets, solar systems, galaxies, and universes. The strange Ariel drawings known as "Ley Lines" presumably direct UFO's to these portals. Some of these drawings are 600 feet across and it is difficult of fathom how such drawings could have been made. Who made these strange drawings, and for what other purpose could they have other than to guide alien spacecraft to our door?

If Earth is being visited by extra-terrestrial beings, even throughout ancient times, it seems unlikely that their intent is to do us

54

harm. Perhaps they are monitoring our technological advancements.
Perhaps they have propelled us along early on, continuing to keep tabs
on us, like mice in a research experiment. They may view Homo
sapiens as a curiosity, wondering if we will ultimately cause our own
demise. Instead of being something to fear, aliens could someday be
our saving grace. Aliens, if they're watching, could save us from
ourselves and from extinction, if they are so inclined. Because UFO
sightings have become more numerous of late, it may indicate that we
are becoming more interesting to them. Maybe alien civilizations
realize humans are at a turning point within their existence.

Alien life forms might not be a threat at all. They may ardently
be waiting to see how our technology unfolds, how humans utilize new
scientific advancements with the intent to steer us away from the
subsequent control of these technologies. More frequent extra-
terrestrial visits could indicate that humans are drawing ever closer to
either a type 11 civilizations or extinction. Depending on how we
handle the new technologies that we develop and whether we allow
these technologies to control us, could make all the difference.

Adapt or Die

"Intelligence is the ability to adapt to change."
--Stephen Hawking

On Earth every living thing must adapt to the changes within its environment or it will die. The intelligence that is required to adapt to change is innate in all species. It is the force that steers evolution. Every adaptation helps organisms survive in their own ecological niche. An adaptive trait, which has evolved by means of natural selection over time, contributes to the fitness and survival of that species. Over time, if the environment changes little, the species comes to fit its surroundings better and better. However, if changes in the environments occur rapidly, the species becomes less and less adaptive.

Some species change physically to accommodate their habitat, in astonishing ways. The marine iguana developed a short, stubby snout to feed on algae off underwater rocks in the ocean. When food is scarce it shrinks by consuming its own bones to survive. When food is again plentiful, the iguana grows back to its original adult length. Even household pets such as, dogs and cats adapt to changes in temperature by growing lush fur in the winter and shedding their fur when the temperature rises.

For Homo sapiens it is our intelligence that has given us the edge over other species. Humans have learned how to adapt. We have built structures, planted crops, invented machines and developed and harnessed energy. Humans have domesticated animals and discovered fire. We created clothing and shoes to protect our bodies and heating and air conditioning to adjust to temperature changes.

In the past when Homo sapiens needed to adapt, we invented a solution for the problem. It's because humans can change easily, that chemicals, toxins and other stimuli introduced into our environment can affect us, sometimes without our knowledge of their presence. The more pesticides and chemicals we throw into our environment the harder it will be for humans and other species to adapt to. As the Earth warms, environmental conditions may be changing too quickly even for humans to adapt to. Changes that happen too quickly leave less time for species to adapt, threatening them with extinction.

The rapid loss of species we are seeing today has been estimated as between 1,000 to 10,000 times higher than the natural extinction rate. The natural extinction rate is the rate of species extinction that would occur if humans were not around. This estimate offers reliable evidence of our swiftly changing environment. There is an intimate connection between other species and us. It is not only our physical environment but also the intrinsically dynamic of the life and death of all living things that can ultimately change the trajectory of our existence. With the predicted loss of thousands and thousands of other species, how will that affect human survival?

Today humans are manipulating natural selection. We are intrusively altering the DNA of species; propagating species that Earth has never seen before. Scientist in the field of genetics may have had good intentions, such as feeding an overpopulated world, but has recklessly forgotten sufficient testing for safety. This is a pattern that happens when human greed is involved. This pattern is obvious again and again, whenever new scientific discoveries are made. For example, if a natural substance were discovered that could cure cancer, it would be of little interest to pharmaceutical companies because they wouldn't be able to patent it.

New scientific advancements spawn synthetic organisms, which own characteristics that are from an unnatural origin. Humans have begun to tamper with nature on a paramount scale in many areas. We have gone past the point of genetic engineering to re-engineering. Companies such as Monsanto are determined to control the seeds of the world with their 'terminator seed' but that's only the tip of iceberg.

Most of us would be stunned to know of how far bioscience is willing to go with new DNA technology. Science can isolate single genes and change the biological properties that exist in any living thing, even other living things in any other world. We are exploring uncharted areas in so many arenas. Man has patented fish that glow, fluorescent colors and bugs that are genetically modified to eat agricultural waste, excreting diesel fuel.

Science may soon be capable of resurrecting the wooly mammoth with DNA plucked from the cells of their frozen carcasses. While scientist claim it is impossible to resurrect the dinosaurs that went extinct 65 million years ago, it is possible to create new ones. Scientists may not be able to bring back the dinosaur precisely, but they can sure manufacture a close second.

The "resurrection" is based on the creation of a hybrid embryo. Dinosaur DNA that is fully preserved could theoretically be implanted into a species that is a descendent of the dinosaur. The result would not be a known dinosaur species but a totally different kind of dinosaur. This kind of tampering with natural selection is similar to every other genetically modified thing that is being created by splicing genes and injecting genes of another species. It's a totally new species.

In the UK genetically modified babies is poised to become a reality. A new form of IVF treatment, which uses the DNA from three parents, may soon become legally available to couples. This new procedure is designed to eliminate genetic mutation that can lead to blindness, and epilepsy as well as other medical problems. If Parliament votes the procedure into law, the UK would be the first to allow pre-birth human DNA modification.

Humans have already dabbled into cloning living things. The first mammal to be cloned was Dolly the sheep in 2003. Since the cloning began, we have cloned a large assortment of animals. We have cloned: cats, dogs, cattle, carp, deer, rabbits, frogs, fruit flies, mice, wolves, water buffalo and Rhesus monkeys.

When George W. Bush was President he passed into law the "Newborn Screening Saves Lives Act." This law requires that hospital collect the DNA of all newborn babies. The DNA is to be stored as government property in bio banks for use in genetic experiments. The collection of babies' DNA is done without parental consent and allows the Government to use it for whatever purposes it wants.

Some believe that the destiny of human's survival lies in the ability to incorporate humans with machines. Followers on this path point to the exponential growth of computers and their capacity. It is assumed that computers and technology will surpass the human brain in the very near future. The point when artificial intelligence surpasses human intelligence is known as the singularity. It is at this point in our evolution that radical changes in civilization will be imminent.

We have already inadvertently ventured ever closer to machines in many realms. New medical innovations have extended life expectancy with landmark breakthroughs. Homo sapiens can generate new, spare body parts with the aid of stem cells. A new organ can be cultivated by utilizing the scaffold of an organ and inserting one's own genes. The result is a new organ that is designed to 'fit' without the possibility of body rejection. This is an amazing demonstration of human adaptability.

Humans in one short jump, have extended life expectancy another quarter of a century. Some scientists believe we may even technologically expect to extend live expectancy indefinitely, in the near future. Science insinuates that if we unlock the secrets of DNA we can rebuild whatever we want. And humans are nothing if not imaginative creatures. We are in fact, the imagination of ourselves.

What we can imagine we can become. The only question is whether or not we will be satisfied as to what science allows us to become.

Nanotecnology

"In contrast with our intellect, computers double their performance every 18 months. So the danger is real that they could develop intelligence and take over the world."
--Stephen Hawking

A powerful new technology has arrived which is setting the stage for some dramatic changes here on Earth. It has caused us to embark on inventions that have the potential to shake up all previous notions of what our world is. It is through the study of the tiny that humans are altering life, as we know it. Nanotechnology is the new technology that allows science to take apart and reconstruct nature at the molecular level. Nanotechnology has become increasingly important in society because it enables materials to become stronger and more effective.

Most of the general public is unaware how prevalent nanotechnology already is in our everyday lives. Its applications touch a variety of industries including computers, mobile phones, pharmaceutical drugs and even food. Nanoparticles can be found in cosmetics, aluminum foil, non-stick cookware, sunscreen, food additives and vitamin supplements. Humans are devouring 10 trillion nanoparticles a day. Still with thousands of products being ingested or applied to the skin, there is no evidence that nanoparticles can be absorbed or metabolized by the human body. It has been estimated that by the year 2015 some $2.6 trillion worth of nanotechnology manufactured foods will be sold each year.

The FDA has not regulated the use of nanoparticles in food and an assortment of other products but studies have shown that nanometer-diameter particles were capable of crossing the brain barrier and into the brain of rats. Some studies have found that nanoparticles may cause toxic and harmful effects. Nanoparticles are able to move through cellular membranes and past the body's defenses with ease. In short, few studies have observed how these particles affect the whole organism. Why is this significant? It's because once again humans have put the cart before the horse. Whilst the general populace is virtually unaware of its dangers, nanotechnology could turn out to be a ticking time bomb with new products being developed as we speak.

Nanorobotics is the emerging technology that is capable of creating machines or robots whose components are at or close to the scale of a nanometer. Nanorobots are being designed ranging from 0.1-10 micrometers in size. Some of these may be primitive molecular machines but they have many practical applications. Richard Feynman and his former graduate student and collaborator Albert Hibbs suggested that micromachines, which could repair machines, might one day be reduced to the size that it would be possible, in theory, to "swallow the doctor." Today this prediction has become a reality.

The "Smart Pill" is a noteworthy advancement in nanotechnology that is in essence, like swallowing your doctor. The smart pill can do much more than deliver drugs to the patient. These pills monitor the health status of patients with sensors that are barely a millimeter thick. The tiny sensors in these pills signal heart rate, temperature and alert your physician when you missed a dose of medication. Smart pills can be programmed, instructed and directed to certain parts of the body. They are the new microelectromechanical system that takes us to another level in medical science. Smart pills can be used to deliver drugs to a certain target or perform surgeries that eliminate the complexity and trauma of cutting the body from the outside.

The smart pill is akin to microchip technology. Microchips have been used on dogs and cats for identification purposes. Unfortunately, the permanently implanted microchips have displayed some troubling results such as cancers, disabilities and death. The Veri Chip, which is being considered for human use, is almost identical to the ones for canines. Scientific studies on permanently implanted microchips on humans that store medical data about them cause cancer in 1-10% of mice and rats. Even if proponents of microchips proclaim they don't fix to any one-body part, the real danger is in the constant exposure. Whatever the risk of smart pills and microchips, one undeniable fact is they have begun the revolution of the nanorobot.

Nanorobots will be the new microscopic assassins of the body's diseases. Prototypes of Nanorobots have shown they have the ability to kill cancer cells by either heating them up or vibrating the cell. A doctor practicing nanomedicine could simply inject a cancer patient with a special type of nanorobot that would seek out cancer cells and destroy them. If all goes as planned the patient would be unaware of the molecular device at work inside, only noticing the betterment of their health.

Other small wonders of technology could come in the form of prosthetic devices. A Denmark man, who lost his hand, had electrodes surgically implanted in his nerves while a prosthetic hand was connected. Now he is able to feel again. According to Silvestro Micera, a researcher who worked on the project, "The idea was to translate the language of the prosthetic into an electrical signal the central nervous system could understand." These results do more than expanding the possibilities for amputees, they are indicative of the direction science and nanotechnology is taking us.

Within the past decade medical science has fit more than eleven million people worldwide with artificial body parts. There are body parts being grown in petri dishes, titanium hearts ready for transplant, synthetic corneas being manufactured and mechanical hands and legs being attached to the human form. As science and technology creates computer chips that are tinier and more powerful, engineers are fitting them with biological sensors, electrodes, and radio receivers. New devices and innovations are tapping directly into the senses and reaching deep inside the brain itself.

The ancient Chinese were the first to discover that the human body was run by an electrical current. Over the last century scientists have forged ahead to tap into this electrical system to restore lost functions and repair the body, as if it were a machine. Through advancements in nanotechnology we may be creating the future of our species. Soon the frailties of the human species, our failing sight, our broken limbs, and the crippling limitations of illness and age will become obsolete. While some of these breakthroughs appear to be life saving, other aspects remain steeped in uncertainty as to where they will lead us.

Human to Machine

"As the computational power to emulate the human brain becomes available—we're not there yet, but we will be there within a couple of decades—projects already under way to scan the human brain will be accelerated, with a view both to understand the human brain in general, as well as providing a detailed description of the contents and design of specific brains. By the third decade of the twenty-first century, we will be in a position to create highly detailed and complete maps of all relevant features of all neurons, neural connections and synapse in the human brain, all of the neural details that play a role in the behavior and functionality of the brain, and to recreate these designs in suitably advanced neural computers."
--Ray Kurzweil

Can Homo sapiens circumvent mortality and avoid the extinction of his own species by engineering a new race of people? Is the future of humans entering a new era of silicon and steel? The electrical current that flows through our nerves cells and neurons carry instructions and information but will this current someday travel to man-made parts?

As our machines become more human, we edge ever closer to integrating these new mechanical parts with the human body. We are undeniably drawing closer to the day when we will become cybernetic organism. Futurists of the past have imagined that our technology could one day alter the course of human evolution and redesign the species. Have humans found a way to manipulate evolution and survive our changing environment through technology? What will the future hold for humanoids with chip implanted brains and wired torsos?

While the human form is being redesigned to be stronger, faster and smarter, robots are being built with high tech vision recognition and motor coordination systems that will mimic human abilities. Humanoid robots that mimic facial expressions and lip movements and appear to show emotional responses will become robotic companions that care for children and the elderly or accompany astronauts into space. In the not so distant future robots will be able to do all the mundane, repetitive and dangerous jobs that humans don't want to do. Robots have come a-long-way-baby. Scientists have engineered the first 'cyborg' tissue—which uses living human cells and organic polymers. It is a combination of neurons, heart cells and nanoelectronic wiring. The lab grown flesh merges tissue with electronics in a way that it becomes difficult to determine where the tissue ends and the electronics begin.

Who would have thought that robots could imitate humans in such detail? Since science has figured out how to produce electricity from decaying organic matter, we have created robots that can convert food into electricity and eliminate their own waste. One day, robot technology will become so humanistic that a robot's responses will be the same as that of humans.

Enterprises that are interested and investing in new technologies such as: bioacoustic sensing devices quantified self, 3D bioprinting, human augmentation, brain-computer interface, speech-to-speech translation, augmented reality and gesture control—culminate technology for financial reasons. Replacing humans in certain jobs will become the norm, as the new robotic workers will do all unpleasant or dangerous jobs without complaint.

As the technology between humans and machines integrates, the line of what is human is starting to blur. Will humans merge peacefully with the robots we build, or will they someday surpass our intelligence and abilities to such an extent that they demand their own rights? Perhaps if this is the route Homo sapiens choose for the future we will become second class citizens that are ruled by our robot counter partners.

As a species, humans must adapt or die, to the changing environment we are creating. If we can't fix what is wrong with our environment we must then fix ourselves so we can somehow survive a toxic planet. We can become 'human part 2' who has rewired their body parts and replaced their heart with nuclear fuel cells. If there's no food available, no problem—the lab can cook something up, perhaps a pill for dinner. A parched Earth that is absent of vegetation, crustaceans and animals with not much available water, wouldn't matter much to a cyborg anyway. As humans embrace new technologies that will free the human body of its' frailties, our biological parts will be replaced with mechanical parts. How will we feel about our new reality? It will certainly be different from anything we as humans, have ever known.

Gradually, we will make the shift to transform ourselves. Virtual reality and computers are soon to become fashion statements as we waltz through life with computer assembled on our sunglasses or wristwatches. Meanwhile, science and technology doesn't stop. In short, evolution doesn't stop either. By evolutionary standards, a few hundred years is only a mere blink of the eye. The transition from humans to cyborgs, albeit gradual, is exactly where our technology is leading us to.

But if this is where we are headed to as a species, will we enjoy our future? If becoming cyborgs enables us to extend life indefinitely, will we be happy with our new existence? Is the future human existence pre-destined to evolve into cybernetic organisms? In this way we may escape the fate of other species that have gone extinct before us.

But if we choose this route, will we pine for the good old days? Will we look through aged picture books to reminisce about the time when Earth had plants and animals on it? Will we someday fondly remember species that have since gone extinct? What will the future feel like for humans turned cyborg?

We may find the consequences of our past too depressing. On the other hand, as cyborgs, the loss of our indigenous world might not bother us much. Nobody knows if cyborgs have feelings of remorse or feelings at all. If we have any indication that something is phonetically wrong with our new reality, then conceivably we could elevate the problem with a slight adjustment. Maybe all we'd need is some new brain circuitry installed or a quick zap to the frontal lobe, to forget such horrific memories.

Although the wave of technology points in the direction of humans becoming cyborgs as the most likely solution to avoid extinction, it is not the only choice. There is one more option for mankind but this option will require adaptation as well. If humans can't fix what's wrong here on Earth and we can't fix ourselves to adapt to it, our only other option is to escape Earth.

Escaping Earth

"Our only chance to long term survival, is not to remain inward looking on planet Earth, but to spread out into space."
--Stephen Hawkins

Here we are at door number two. This is our last option to avoid extinction as a species. If we cannot fix what things are broken on planet Earth and we are unable or unwilling to adapt to what is prevalent here, then we must flee. As one of the greatest physicists and cosmologists Stephen Hawking has warned humans: extinction is on the horizon. While Earth is not necessarily a delicate planet, humans continue to batter it persistently. Hawking said, "We must continue to go into space for humanity. We won't survive another 1,000 years without escaping our fragile planet."

It seems almost unimaginable how the life that we have grown accustomed to would be continued on Mars. Most scientists, who believe that interplanetary colonization is the next frontier for humans, agree that Mars would be the place that holds the most potential. Mars is the closest planet to Earth and scientists contend that at one time it was very similar to Earth. Today, there is evidence that two billion years ago Mars was a much warmer and wetter place than it is today. Frozen Martian rivers foretell a distant past that parallels that of our Earth. Scientists who are proponents of humans becoming a space faring species claim Mars has all the resources we need to support life and a technological civilization. Besides water, it has carbon and nitrogen. It has mineral ore stored within its complex geology, which alludes to the conclusion, that there are available sources of geothermal energy. Mars even has 24-hour days, which will be an important factor in creating a fertile environment for plant life.

For all the similarities that scientists identify between Mars and Earth there are many problems that we would encounter when colonizing the red planet. Terraforming Mars would need to be done in stages with the primary issue being the temperature of Mars. Of course we would need to warm it up and if humans know how to do anything its how to create greenhouse gasses. We are practicing this today as the greenhouse effect builds in our atmosphere and attempts to sizzle the planet Earth. While global warming and climate change is feared here on Earth, for Mars it would be the desired result. In theory, we could create the greenhouse effect on Mars by trapping 10% of the sunlight or photons that hit Mars. By that timeframe it is estimated that Mars would warm up significantly within 100 years. As more and more of these greenhouse gasses become trapped in the atmosphere the planets temperature would eventually stabilize—staying warm naturally. Now colonists could walk around the planet unencumbered with spacesuits.

Of course we would still have the problem of breathing, so carrying an oxygen tank around would be necessary. But scientists insist this problem would be resolved too, as the frozen rivers and seas melt, allowing humans to bring simple organisms from Earth to begin the process of initiating life on Mars. After a while, more complex plants could be introduced and they would be right at home in this carbon dioxide atmosphere. Soon they would begin to flourish and transform Mars into a green world similar to Earth. The process of plant growth, photosynthesis and oxygen could take near a thousand years to create but it would bring an atmosphere that would be suitable for humans.

Terraforming Mars would take awhile. That's why governments that see Mars as a viable option for humans are starting to ramp up now. Attempts to go to Mars have been made since the 1960's by the United States, Russia, Europe and Japan with the U.S. having already had many successful missions. We have successfully deposited cameras, lasers, spectrometers and radar systems on Mars, now NASA and President Obama wants to send astronauts to Mars by 2030.

There have also been several private space flight projects proposed. One such project is Mars One, which is a project that is led by Dutch entrepreneur, Bas Lansdorp. Mars One is a not-for-profit foundation that plans to establish a permanent human colony on Mars by 2023. According to plans to colonize Mars groups of four astronauts will be chosen to take a one way trip to Mars and begin the colonization process. So far some 200,000 people have signed up for the registration of their one way ticket.

Another initiative is Mars to Stay, which astronauts such as Buzz Aldren argue that its boarders should envision their sojourn as that of pioneers, not so different from that of the pilgrims. The idea of sending astronauts to Mars, never to return, might sound unsettling at first but as Physicist Lawrence Krauss puts it, "To boldly go where no one has gone before does not require coming home again."

Yet another ambitious plan to colonize Mars comes from Elon Musk, billionaire and founder of SpaceX. Musk estimates the trip to the Mars would cost around $500,000 to shuttle some 80,000 settlers to Mars. However, the plan does have some contingencies. It must develop reusable rockets that are able to take off and land vertically and would begin with smaller groups of colonists, until life is more sustainable. Although Musk is hoping to have the first stage version of the rocket ready by 2018, he admits it could take longer.

Another billionaire, Dennis Tito is also planning to launch a manned mission to Mars in 2017 but that would only be a flyby that will exploit the rare alignment of Mars and Earth in order to save travel time and fuel. Its mission would provide a bird's eye view of Mars, as the rocket sails within 100 feet from the surface.

Perhaps the most logical plan for colonizing the red planet may be the ideas being initiated by the World's Space Agencies, which propose a joint endeavor manned Mars Mission. Through this agency, 12 national space agencies are developing the roadmap for humans to inhabit Mars. Countries such as the U.S., Japan, China, Russia and the European Union are intent on advance space exploration and the colonization of Mars by the 2030's. Not only can these nations share their knowledge but also the cost for a mission to Mars. It would make perfect sense for all space faring nations to put their heads together in an effort to save the species. Sending a rocket full of pioneers to Mars is one thing but keeping them alive quite another.

Issues such as radiation and zero gravity would need to be worked out as well. Radiation is seen as the biggest hurdle of space travel with the maximum time in space being one year before dangerously high radiation doses are accumulated within the body. Some deliberate the odds of cancer from the radiation of space travel as being only slightly elevated. Data gathered by NASA and the Curiosity Rover suggests that astronauts could endure a six-month flight, 600-day stay on Mars, and the six-month journey home without accumulating high doses of radiation.
This is a theory that is not yet proven. Still NASA and others are feverish studying the psychological and physiological effects of long-term space travel. In order to counter the risk of radiation we need to be able to build rockets that are more protective to its passengers.

All of the large and minute problems that go with becoming a multi-planet species or escaping the Earth altogether, could one day be conquered if we collectively work for solutions. We could then go to Mars. Collectively as a species we could become more machine like or we can simply fix what we have broken here. As astrophysicist Neal deGrasse Tyson says, "It's a very simple argument. If we have the power to convert Mars into something that looks like Earth, then we have the power to fix our own oceans and our own atmosphere, right? If you have the power of geo-engineering, you don't have to leave the planet you're on, turn another one into Earth, and move there. Just fix Earth."

It's smart to cover as many of the bases as possible and to have multiple plans; just in case. Homo sapiens are the species that has evolved to own a big brain. We have come a very long way in a relatively short time. We have shown how adaptive we can be but are we smart enough to avoid our own extinction? Science, technology and research will never stop, and nor should it.

Nations across the planet are wising up to the consequences we will soon be facing. The combination of climatic and environmental disturbances could easily do us in, as well as any number of outside forces. As a species we have forged ahead when challenged by environmental changes. We somehow found ways to deal with the bad situations. We did this through communication, collaboration with others and through our inventions.

Before our intellect developed we had instinctive qualities that were as important as the size of our brains. These instincts bonded us together as a species and allowed us to survive. These are instincts such as mothers' love, compassion and cooperation. As our frontal lobes grew, we learned we could do thing better when we cooperated with one another. We learned we could survive by using our conjoined knowledge.

It is said the evolution is a continuing process. We might not be aware of changes that are happening because of our limited perspective. Because evolution is a slow process we may not notice changes happening right before our eyes. Are Homo sapiens losing one of his most important attributes—the ability to cooperate in order to solve problems?

Whatever we become and where ever we go we must remember how we got where we are today. We must recall our most basic instincts and connect to our collective intelligence. Whether humans will evolve into machine like creatures or become a space faring species may not depend on what is in our DNA or what is the best end result. Homo sapiens are the only species that realizes that we all someday will die. As we float through space and time, on one small, blue planet, our destiny remains a blank slate for our descendents to fashion and determine. Our future as a species is what it has always been; we are the imagination of ourselves.

About the Author

Renee Rotto was born in Chicago, Illinois. After moving to Daytona Beach, Florida with her family, she attended Daytona Beach State College where she embarked on a journey of extensive research on environmental issues. She has written numerous articles about the dangers of our changing environment, including online sources such as: Helium, Hubpages and Bubblews. The systematic search for truth and facts has led her to some serious and sensitive conclusions about the fate of humans as a species. Questions remain about the devastating changes of climate change, overpopulation, and pollution and how they will alter life on planet Earth.

Science is changing our scope of understanding the meaning of life. Physics is probing new wide-ranging theories with the inference that humans are indeed connected to every other living thing. Renee Rotto believes it is only through taking responsibility for the guardianship of our planet and creatures that human beings will begin to control their own destiny. She is a believer of the miracle of life. It is because all living things cling to life with the intention of thriving as a species. Renee genuinely trusts that Homo sapiens have the innate ability to confront unlimited obstacles, and that somehow even within the most desperate of times, it is still possible to turn things around.

www.ingramcontent.com/pod-product-compliance
Lightning Source LLC
Chambersburg PA
CBHW080434290526
45791CB00008BA/2501